Alan: Happy quarter of a cent...!
Hope y...
Cam... ...as!
... ...nine.

Many happy returns

Tim
&
Wendy

Cambridge: March 1977

Leavis

LEAVIS

Ronald Hayman

HEINEMANN
London
ROWAN AND LITTLEFIELD
Totowa, New Jersey

Heinemann Educational Books Ltd
LONDON EDINBURGH MELBOURNE TORONTO
AUCKLAND SINGAPORE HONG KONG
KUALA LUMPUR IBADAN NAIROBI
JOHANNESBURG LUSAKA
NEW DELHI KINGSTON

ISBN (U.K.) 0 435 18452 0
ISBN (U.S.A.) 0-87471-917-8

Published in Great Britain by
Heinemann Educational Books Ltd
48 Charles Street, London W1X 8AH
First published in the United States 1976 by
Rowan and Littlefield, Totowa, New Jersey
Printed in Great Britain by
Cox & Wyman Ltd, London, Fakenham and Reading

Contents

Acknowledgments

That I am grateful to Dr Leavis does not go without saying but there is the whole book to say it. I am also grateful to Ian Hamilton, editor of *The New Review*. I had written profiles of Tom Stoppard and Claude Chabrol for him before contributing an article on *The Calendar of Modern Letters* to his series *The Little Magazines*. The two lines converged in my next suggestion, that I should write about Dr Leavis. Ian's response was to offer me unlimited space. Though the resulting essay was longer than anything that had previously appeared in *The New Review*, it was not long enough to incorporate the criticism I wanted to write of Leavis's criticism. The ratio of criticism to biography is therefore much higher in the book than it was in the essay, but, apart from drawing on the letters that Dr Leavis, Lord Annan and Professor Henri Fluchère wrote to *The Times Literary Supplement* to correct a few factual errors, I have retained virtually everything I originally wrote.

I am extremely grateful for the conversations which combined with what Dr Leavis had written about himself to give me my first biographical footholds. Those who were kind enough to talk to me about him included Philip Brockbank, William Empson, Boris Ford, Andor Gomme, R. T. Jones, Graham Martin, John Newton, W. W. Robson, Leo Salingar, Geoffrey Strickland, Martin Turnell and Eric Warmington. I received helpful letters from Ronald Bottrall and Denys Thompson, and I should like to thank Philip French for letting me see a transcript of the interviews he did for his Radio 3 commemoration of Dr Leavis's eightieth birthday. A special word of gratitude is due to Graham Martin for encouraging me to think not just of an essay but of a book. R.H.

The author and publishers gratefully acknowledge the copyright-holders' permission to include quotations from the works of F. R. Leavis, F. R. Leavis and Denys Thompson, and Q. D. Leavis. These copyright-holders are the authors and Chatto & Windus in the case of *Revaluation, Culture and Environment*, and *Education and the University* throughout the world; the author and Chatto & Windus (Barnes & Noble in the U.S.A.) in the case of *Nor Shall My Sword*; and the author and Chatto & Windus (Pantheon Books in the U.S.A.) in the case of *Two Cultures?*, *Anna Karenina*, and *Dickens the Novelist*. The author and publishers also wish to thank Faber & Faber and Harcourt, Brace Jovanovich (in the U.S.A.) for permission to quote extracts from *Four Quartets* by T. S. Eliot.

FOR MY MOTHER

Whoever sets himself to see things as they are will find himself one of a very small circle; but it is only by this small circle resolutely doing its own work that adequate ideas will ever get current at all.

MATTHEW ARNOLD

'There's a hatred of art, there's a hatred of literature – I mean of the genuine kinds. Oh the shams – those they'll swallow by the bucket!'

The Author in
HENRY JAMES's '*The Author of Beltraffio*'

A great work of art explores and evokes the grounds and sanctions of our most important choices, valuations and decisions – those decisions which are not acts of will, but are so important that they seem to make themselves rather than to be made by us.

F. R. LEAVIS

Introduction

Gas in the First World War, they said, had caused the nasal twang, but his voice, dry and astringent, was at one with his eagle face. In the early fifties he was the only don to wear an open-necked shirt, usually white, under the loose gown hanging like black wings around his bony body. The open collar displayed greying hairs on the lean chest. Larynx, tendons and veins stood out on the creased neck surmounted with clean-cut jaw, precise mouth, aquiline nose, dark, quick, penetrating eyes set deeply in lined flesh, healthily sun-tanned. The firm, round, hard, bald skull was fringed with greying hair that wisped back over the big, sensitive ears.

Some of the dons were performers, unable to disguise their relish for the effects they could produce in the lecture-hall with a histrionic pause following a carefully turned phrase of their own or a carefully selected quotation, recited almost as if they wanted applause. Either Leavis was totally untheatrical or he was giving an incomparably subtler performance. His voice could not have been less actorish and he did not affect an elocutionary tone for reading poetry. Like T. S. Eliot, he read astringently, anti-romantically, not without commitment, not without sustained tone, but rigorously refusing to emote, letting words and rhythms generate their own force.

The sleepier lecturers would read their way through notes that might have been written three years ago for a course that would still be the same three years from now. Leavis seemed to be thinking his way from point to point. Great energy was involved, but it was neither vocal nor physical. It lay behind what he was saying and it must have been this energy that generated the excitement which drew such big audiences. His subject was 'Judgment and Analysis' – he disliked the phrase 'Practical Criticism' – but what he was doing was teaching us how to read. He would distribute passages of verse and prose, and not yet knowing either the author or the period, we would scribble notes in the margin, fully aware that they wouldn't be of much help afterwards, because what was happening was unrepeatable. He was releasing something that had been latent in the printed words on the page, creating a new entity in the lecture-hall, a poem that depended as much on evaluation as interpretation and as much on our presence as on his, its life lodged temporarily in the collective reaction.

Those of us who hadn't taken it for granted that we'd learnt how to read at school had probably bought *On the Art of Reading* by Sir Arthur Quiller-Couch, who had been Regius Professor till 1944. His book, based on lectures he'd given, referred us back to the Bible and the classics, quoting the old schoolmaster who told his English set that 'if they could really master the ninth book of Paradise Lost, so as to rise to the height of its great argument and incorporate all its beauties in themselves, they would at one blow, by virtue of that alone, become highly cultivated men'. Most of us had also spent a lot of time on footnotes in the Arden edition of Shakespeare, on the histories of English literature by George Saintsbury and by Legouis and Cazamian, and on books that packed biographical facts and scholarly comparisons like layer after layer of coloured tissue paper around the precious gift of literary experience. Irreverently Leavis ripped everything out of the way in his eager assault on the words. The facts of Shelley's life were irrelevant to the decision we had to take about whether his poems were good or bad.

It was an enormous relief to learn that a reader had rights and a writer responsibilities. It wasn't my job to conjure up the image of a blithe spirit which had never been a bird and whose heart soared from heaven or near it, unless Shelley used the right words and rhythms to suggest it. And maybe it was Matthew Arnold's fault that I found it so hard to picture a darkling plain where ignorant armies clashed by night. Leavis would read, analyse, isolate images from their context, put them back again, question us about the prose sense of the poem, and answer his own questions, but not before we'd had time to form our own opinions. If the author of the poem that started

Tears idle tears, I know not what they mean

seemed to be inviting us to wallow with him in a tepid bath of undefined emotion, there was no need to talk respectfully about his musicality just because he was Tennyson. Invited to compare the poem, anonymously, with one that started

Softly, in the dusk, a woman is singing to me

most of us probably felt quite willing to agree that this was less self-indulgent and more specific in the pictures it called to mind. Leavis was liberating because he made us feel that nothing mattered except the arrangement of the words on the page, but that mattered enormously because the partnership between writer and reader could be creative. It depended both on the quality of the writing and the quality of the attention we paid to it, and he made us want to emulate him in bringing memory, imagination, sensitivity, moral judgment and taste to bear on the attitudes, ideas and feelings expressed in the words.

He also provided a terminology. The critic's tools were words, and some of his words helped to focus resistances and reservations that might otherwise have stayed below the level of consciousness. 'Plangent' was a good word for the lulling or the lachrymose, and 'afflatus' was valuable for puncturing overblown rhetoric. The most useful words of all were 'intelligence' and 'realize'. Archaisms, alliteration and hypnotic rhythms should not blind us to mindlessness, while the poet, no less than the prose writer, had to make his subject matter real for the reader.

Dr Leavis was also capable of complaining at considerable length about Dame Edith Sitwell and Sir Osbert and Sir Sacheverell, about Mr Alan Pryce Jones and the inadequacy of the *Times Literary Supplement* under his editorship, about the low standard of book-reviewing in the *New Statesman* and the Sunday papers, about the irresponsibility of the British Council and the BBC. He also submitted us to lengthy anecdotes that demonstrated how he had been the victim of misinterpretation and deliberate misrepresentation. Not that he ever indulged in self-pity; he merely wanted us to know how corrupt the cultural Establishment was. What we didn't know was how long he had remained an outsider in the Cambridge English School. After taking his Ph.D. in 1924 he had started lecturing in 1927, but he lost his job in 1931 and stayed defiantly on in Cambridge without being officially reinstated as a university lecturer until 1936. It was not until 1954 that he was invited to become a member of the Faculty Board and he was in his sixty-fifth year when he was appointed to a Readership. He was never offered a Chair at Cambridge.

By the end of this century, perhaps, critics will have begun to find it unnecessary to preface remarks with 'I'm not a Leavisite but . . .' To talk of Leavisites and Anti-Leavisites is, effectively, to deny the fact that he has developed and changed his mind. He is not a system, a creed or a set of abstract principles. The most important function of the critic is to improve the cultural situation by raising the general

level of critical response. His work, therefore, must be largely corrective. In the late twenties and early thirties, when T. S. Eliot and
D. H. Lawrence were still being seriously underrated, Leavis's
campaign for them made an important contribution towards lifting
their reputations to their present level. If Eliot is now being over-
praised, it is his limitations that the critic should emphasize, as
Leavis does, cogently, in his four essays on *Four Quartets* in *The Living
Principle* (1975). Is the 'Anti-Leavisite' critic opposed to what Leavis
wrote in 1932 or to what he wrote in 1975? Or indiscriminately
hostile to everything he says?

A critic, like a teacher, can be understood only by taking account
of the context in which he worked, and for the last fifty years Dr
Leavis has been primarily a teacher. That is one reason for the
semi-biographical approach I have adopted in this book. Good
criticism is almost as worthy as art is of the word 'creative', but most
criticism cannot stand up so well as a work of art to isolation from its
cultural, social and biographical context. Most of Leavis's ideas,
value judgments and opinions were expressed in the supervision room
or the lecture-hall before they were committed in print. His prose
style, with its elaborate qualifications, has been moulded by syntac-
tical habits he developed as a speaker, though the comparison with
Henry James has often been made, and once he received a letter
that culminated in the sentence 'As the years pass I find the elegance
of your writing reminds me more and more of my Uncle Henry'.
His prose is extremely lucid, and those who have never heard him
lecture are more likely to disagree about its elegance than those who
have. His style is the style of a man primarily concerned to achieve
consensus among a particular audience at a particular time.

Cambridge has been the main base for both his teaching and his
writing. His quarterly, *Scrutiny*, could not have been what it was if
it had been published from London or from Oxford. As he said in
the Retrospect he wrote in 1962 for the University Press's 1963 re-
issue of the twenty volumes, 'Only at Cambridge could the idea of
Scrutiny have taken shape, become a formidable life, and maintained
the continuous living force that made it hated and effective ...
Scrutiny started, established itself and survived in spite of Cambridge.'
It is hard to be sure whether Leavis has done more to change
Cambridge than Cambridge has done to change him; it is certain
that each has given the other a great deal.

In my opinion Leavis is the most important critic of this century.

I shall try to substantiate this verdict in my detailed criticism of his criticism, but there are eight points which can be made in summary form at the outset:

1. He provides more help than any other critic in coming to close grips with a text. The ideal critic is the ideal reader, and Leavis reads with enormous concentration and total commitment, using his ear as well as his eye, his memory as well as his judgment. The act of reading becomes more exciting because he prods us into making it a co-operative process in which we bring as much of ourselves as we can to meet as much of the writer as he has put into the words.

2. Leavis's judgment, though fastidious, is usually sound. He has made mistakes and he has hardly kept in touch with developments in literature since 1950, but his mistakes, by and large, have been less serious and less damaging to the corpus of his critical achievement than the mistakes of T. S. Eliot and Ezra Pound were to theirs.

3. Though it is usually considered to be a disadvantage for a critic not to be also a creative writer, I maintain that it is an advantage. The practitioner's main interest in past literature is in its relevance to his own work; the critic's main interest is in its relevance to the contemporary reader.

4. Leavis has done more than any other teacher to win prestige for English studies, and more than any other critic towards establishing revaluations of English literature determining which writers receive most attention.

5. He is our greatest champion of culture and of critical standards. It was natural for Roy Fuller, lecturing as Professor of Poetry at Oxford, to cite him when arguing that there was no need for a graduate of the English School to surrender to 'magazine diversion and gossip-fodder for the relaxed middlebrow' or to 'stroke the egos of those who have given hostages to pop-culture'.

6. Neither a scholar nor a specialist, Leavis has written perceptively about every period of English literature from the Renaissance to the present. Scholarship, like many institutions, tends to work hardest of all towards ensuring its own survival. While the scholar tries to make himself indispensable, the critic should work, as Leavis does, towards the elimination of everything (including himself) that stands between the writer's words and the reader's mind.

7. Leavis hits out hard against the idea (which some of the Struc-
    turalists have now taken over from the Symbolists) that 'art'
    should be kept in a separate compartment from 'life' and judged
    by different standards. Leavis's criticism proves the validity of his
    belief that 'the establishing of the poem (or the novel) is the
    establishing of a value. Any reading of it that takes it as a work
    of art involves an element of implicit valuation. The process,
    the kind of activity of inner response and discipline, by which
    we take possession of the created work is essentially the kind of
    activity that completes itself in a value-judgment.'[1]

8. He has been extraordinarily unconcerned about his prestige, his
    career and his income. He has fought with admirable consistency
    and rare integrity for what he believes to be important.

[1] *English Literature in Our Time and the University.*

1 Schoolboy, Stretcher-bearer, Student

Harry Leavis, his father, owned a Cambridge shop which sold pianos and other musical instruments. He was a sensitive, cultured, deeply musical man, whose son was to retain throughout his life an admiration for his poise and distinction. Readings from Dickens and from Shakespeare were among the family entertainments.

When Frank Leavis was a new-boy at the well regarded local grammar school, the Perse, the other boys were already familiar with his surname from the advertising slogan 'Leavis spells pianos'. The school had two houses for boarders but most of the boys were day-boys. The headmaster, Dr W. H. D. Rouse, was a classicist and an expert on Sanskrit, which he taught at the University from 1903–39. At Perse he developed his 'practice' – he refused to call it a theory – that the dead languages could best be taught in the same way as the living. Teachers were to carry on classroom conversations with their pupils in Latin and classical Greek, resorting as little as possible to explanations in English. Leavis was later to complain 'I have been obliged to compose verse in Latin and even in Greek'. Rouse would also compose Latin and Greek songs for them to sing. What was probably most important to Leavis was the development of a long-lasting capacity to savour the sense of words through their sound.

'The direct method' (as they called it) was also applied to German and French, which were both taught by an Alsatian whose real name was von Glehn, but – anti-German sentiment being so extreme – he preferred to be known as de Glehn. Not much attention was paid to scientific subjects, but English was taught very well by Mr H. Caldwell Cook, a Shakespeare enthusiast who encouraged his pupils to visualize the plays in performance while they were studying the texts. He also organized school productions of scenes from the plays, and on 6 November 1912, Act II of *Macbeth* was performed with F. R. Leavis in the leading part. According to *The Pelican*, the school magazine, he acted 'extremely well' but did not manage vocally to produce the requisite air of mystery and of the supernatural. Two years later his performance in the rugger field was applauded by *The Pelican* without reservations. He was 'the player who has made the greatest progress in a short time; a very hard-working forward, but light'. Professor Eric Warmington, who was then at the school, remembers him as 'a very quiet boy. He always had an introspective look in his eye as though he were taking stock'. And already he was sufficiently interested in literature to take out a subscription to Ford Maddox Hueffer's *English Review*.

He was just nineteen when Britain declared war on the Kaiser's Germany. Not wanting to kill, he became a stretcher-bearer, working with the Friends' Ambulance Unit and carrying – this part of the story is well known – a copy of Milton's poems in his rucksack. What is not so easy to imagine is the daily experience of contact with maimed and bleeding men, who were going to die but needn't have died if there had been more doctors, more nurses, more medical supplies. Meeting trains loaded with wounded soldiers, he had to give as much help and as much reassurance as he could. They were men of his own age. Among them he'd find faces he knew from school and from the town. He has described how 'those innumerable boy-subalterns who figured in the appalling Roll of Honour as "fallen officers" had climbed out and gone forward, playing their part in the attacking wave, to be mown down with the swathes that fell to the uneliminated machine-guns'.

His nightmares took most of the rest-value out of his sleep and he remained intermittently prone to insomnia throughout his life. The effects of these experiences may have been compounded by gas and shell-shock: his digestive system was permanently damaged. He was advised to eat small quantities of food at short intervals but to have little or nothing after four o'clock in the afternoon. At meals away from home he would seem not to be doing much more than toy politely with the food on his plate. Colleagues formed the impression that his main intake of vitamins came from sunshine absorbed on his long walks and while sitting in his glass conservatory.

It took him a long time to recover from the war. 'In those early years after the great hiatus,' he has written, 'as in a dazed and re-tarded way I struggled to achieve the beginnings of the power of articulate thought about literature, it was Santayana – I picked up Logan Pearsall Smith's *Little Essays from the Writings of George Santayana* when it came out – and Matthew Arnold who really counted.' Though influenced by Santayana, he did not feel in sympathy with him. Nor did he receive more than 'a vague and minor stimulus' from his first acquaintance with *The Sacred Wood* after buying a copy in 1920. 'How I came to buy it so soon after the publication I can't now say. I had never heard of Eliot, and I had no more literary sophistication than I had acquired at school before the war. And though I turned the book over a good deal, and no doubt profited, I won't pretend that I absorbed rapidly what it had to give, or that it became for me, after a short acquaintance, decisively formative.'

He had won a scholarship from the Perse School to Emmanuel College, where he read History. He distinguished himself as a middle and long-distance runner. His father's death occurred just before he had to take the examination for the first part of his Tripos. He did badly, getting only an inferior second-class degree, and decided to switch to English.

The Cambridge English School was at a very early stage of its development. There had been a Chair of Anglo-Saxon since 1878, and between 1883 and 1917 English had been available in the Modern and Medieval Languages Tripos, but few undergraduates had opted for it. At Oxford, English Literature had been introduced in 1904, though with a strong bias towards philology and Middle English. At Cambridge the King Edward VII Professorship was founded in 1911, but it was not until 1917 that an English Honours School was established to launch the course on English 'Literature, Life and Thought' from Chaucer onwards. Meanwhile the undergraduate population was changing. It no longer consisted entirely of school-leavers. There were older men, demobilized from the army and navy and disoriented by what they had experienced.

It was not considered necessary for lecturers in English Literature to have any qualifications in the subject. The most inspired and inspiring of them, Mansfield Forbes, was a historian with a classical background and a passionate interest in the arts. In 1919 he was lecturing on ideas of childhood and parenthood in Blake and Wordsworth. As Joan Bennett has recalled,[1] 'He was developing a theory that words in poems had not only an exact stress and time (indicated by the metre, the rhythm and the sense), but that one must also discover a right pitch of voice for certain key words. Once, after I. A. Richards's return to Cambridge, he and Forbes tried out this theory in a lecture. Each of them gave a viva voce rendering of D. H. Lawrence's poem "Piano" ... To demonstrate his theory about pitch Forbes read in a falsetto voice the word "poised" in the line

[1] Reuben A. Brower, Helen Vendler and John Hollander (eds.), *I. A. Richards. Essays in His Honour*. Oxford University Press 1973.

"And pressing the small poised feet . . ."; his idea was, perhaps, that this would illustrate the weightlessness of feet merely touching the pedals. The effect, however, was irresistibly comic.'

It was Forbes who had been responsible for the appointment of I. A. Richards as a lecturer in English. His training had been in philosophy. In 1915 he graduated from Magdalene with a First in Moral Sciences. He returned in 1921 to stay until 1939, exerting both on the English school and on Leavis an influence which cannot be denied the word 'formative'. In January 1922 Richards began his first course on the novel, and in the autumn he started lecturing on the Theory of Criticism, developing the ideas he was to expound in the book, *Principles of Literary Criticism*, which was published in 1925.[1] It dealt an effective blow to the aestheticism that was still being trumpeted in the phrases 'Art for Art's sake' and 'Poetry for Poetry's sake'. Richards applied a psychological analysis to the stimuli provided by art, arguing that they were not intrinsically different from stimuli given by other varieties of experience. Works of art should therefore be judged not by special 'aesthetic' criteria but by the same moral standards that were applied to everything else.

It is undeniable that Leavis later added a great deal to the ideas he took from Richards; it is also undeniable that he took a great many. He benefited from Richards's analysis of metre and its effects, from the emphasis he put on the value of irony, and from his treatment of sentimentality and facile appeals to stock responses in the reader. Richards must also have catalysed Leavis's interest in Matthew Arnold and T. S. Eliot, while Richards's fears of a cultural collapse may have been seminal. His lectures must have revealed the preoccupations he was to express in Chapter V of *Principles of Literary Criticism*:

> With the increase of population the problem presented by the gulf between what is preferred by the majority and what is accepted as excellent by the most qualified opinion has become infinitely more serious and appears likely to become threatening in the near future. For many reasons standards are much more in need of defence than they used to be. It is perhaps premature to envisage a collapse of values, a transvaluation by which popular taste replaces trained discrimination. Yet commercialism has done stranger things: we have not yet fathomed the more sinister potentialities of the cinema and the loudspeaker, and there is some evidence, uncertain and slight no doubt, that such things

[1] By Routledge and Kegan Paul.

as 'best-sellers' (compare *Tarzan* with *She*), magazine verses, mantelpiece pottery, Academy pictures, Music Hall songs, County Council buildings, War Memorials . . . are decreasing in merit. Notable exceptions, in which the multitude are better advised than the experts, of course occur sometimes, but not often.

Mrs Q. D. Leavis quotes the last sentence in her book *Fiction and the Reading Public*, which had been written as a thesis under Richards's supervision. Explaining in her Introduction how she 'became interested in the general question: What has happened to fiction and the reading public since the eighteenth century?' she goes on to acknowledge: 'I found encouragement to pursue this kind of interest in certain hints thrown out by Mr I. A. Richards in *Principles of Literary Criticism*.' She had taken First Class Honours in the Tripos examination of 1928 and she wrote the thesis after she had been awarded an Ottilie Hancock research fellowship at Girton. The Vice-Mistress, Hilda Murray, had been particularly encouraging. The Leavises were married in 1929. His Ph.D. thesis, which had been finished five years earlier, under the supervision of Sir Arthur Quiller-Couch, had focused on the same process of cultural decline. His title had been *The Relationship of Journalism to Literature: Studied in the Rise and Earlier Development of the Press in England*. The first of its seven chapters had been on 'The Age of Elizabeth: The Beginnings of Journalism' and the fourth was about 'The Growth of a Reading Public.' It may have been Richards who first made him want to concern himself with the relationship between the debasement of cultural standards and the widening of literacy after the Shakespearean period. The preoccupation is central to *Fiction and the Reading Public*, which was published in 1932, to *Scrutiny* which continued from 1932 to 1953, and to Leavis's cultural criticism, from *Mass Civilization and Minority Culture* (1930) to *Nor Shall My Sword* (1972).

The distinction Richards drew between technical and evaluative criticism was also to have its effect on Leavis, but most important of all were the Practical Criticism courses that Richards started in 1925, publishing the results in his book *Practical Criticism* (1929). If an average audience consisted of sixty people, this might include as many as twenty friends, lecturers, graduates and research students, including F. R. Leavis and William Empson, Richards's most brilliant student, who had come up from Winchester to read Mathematics, transferring to English for the second part of the Tripos. He developed his book *Seven Types of Ambiguity* out of essays written for his weekly supervisions at Magdalene. At the Practical Criticism classes Richards would give out printed sheets grouping four or five poems without titles, dates or the authors' names. Members of the audience would have a week to produce 'protocols' describing their reactions to the poems. These would be analysed in class. The names of the poets would then be disclosed but the anonymity of the embarrassed critics was preserved. Richards's friend T. S. Eliot contributed at least one protocol, and the book contains the earliest extant examples of published criticism by Leavis, including some comments on D. H. Lawrence's poem 'Piano', which he was later to use in his own classes on Practical Criticism. Apart from this, Leavis was to publish nothing until he was thirty-two. It was the idea of teaching, not writing, that attracted him.

Leavis's career as a don began auspiciously with a commission to lecture on a freelance basis. In 1927 there were twelve fully-fledged lecturers in English Literature, including Forbes, Richards, Hilda Murray (daughter of Sir James Murray, editor of the *Oxford English Dictionary*), the medievalist G. G. Coulton, his ex-pupil H. S. Bennett, and E. M. W. Tillyard, who had also been at the Perse. He was Leavis's senior by six years and soon to become his arch-enemy. As more undergraduates were opting to read English, more freelance lecturers were employed until, in 1927, Leavis was appointed as one of six Probationary Faculty Lecturers in English – a position later classified as that of Assistant Lecturer.

With his strong sense of mission, Leavis had to do everything in his power to orient students towards the best modern literature, weaning them away from the second-rate. But other lecturers were recommending the literature that was in vogue, including the poetry of Laurence Binyon, Robert Bridges, A. E. Housman, John Masefield, James Elroy Flecker, Edith Sitwell, Walter de la Mare, Siegfried Sassoon and Rupert Brooke. De la Mare and Sassoon were also admired as prose-writers, together with Arnold Bennett, J. M. Barrie, Bernard Shaw, H. G. Wells, Osbert Sitwell, Aldous Huxley, C. E. Montague and Charles Morgan.

Leavis would have been behaving unconscientiously and uncharacteristically if he had failed to put undergrauduates on their guard against current valuations, and how could he do that without criticizing those who subscribed to them? His colleagues were naturally upset to learn of the way their names were being mentioned in his lectures, and one of his broadsides was delivered against Sir Arthur Quiller-Couch's anthology *The Oxford Book of English Verse*, which had been published in 1900, before his appointment to the Cambridge Chair. Personally 'Q' was not in the least offended by Leavis's animadversions against his taste in poetry. He admired the depth of Leavis's commitment to his critical standards and he did not have a high regard for most of the other lecturers. But he spent relatively little time in Cambridge and he had less executive power than the Chairman and Secretary of the Faculty Board.

It was obvious to Leavis that the best living prose writers were James Joyce and D. H. Lawrence, but they were both outsiders, condemned as obscene by a great many people who hadn't read them. In 1925, when Leavis had been giving a course of lectures on English prose, *Ulysses*, which had been published in Paris three years previously, was not on sale in the English bookshops, though copies that had been smuggled into the country were circulating among undergraduates. Lawrence's books were in the English Faculty library but the librarian had been instructed not to let undergraduates borrow them or even read them in the library. Taking the advice of his bookseller, Leavis wrote to the Home Office for permission to import a copy of *Ulysses*, but instead of a reply to his application he received an invitation to call on the Vice-Chancellor of the university, Professor Seward, who was also Master of Downing College. Arriving at the Master's Lodge, Leavis was surprised to be handed a lengthy typescript from the Public Prosecutor's Office. It incorporated a report provided by the Cambridge police on Leavis and his lectures, giving details of the average attendance and the proportion of women in the audience. *Ulysses* was characterized as 'indescribably filthy'. 'We do not suppose you have read it, and shall be pleased to send you a copy for examination.' Assuming that Leavis wanted the book to be prescribed for the English Tripos, the Public Prosecutor suggested that he should be suitably and firmly dealt with.

To defend himself he made the point to the Vice-Chancellor that the furtive reading of smuggled copies was not conducive to serious study. What he wanted to eliminate was 'the glamour of the clandestine attending the cult'. He added: 'I could easily have got a copy by letting myself be put in touch with one of the disreputable agents every bookseller knows of.'

'I'm glad you didn't do that,' said the Professor. 'Letters get intercepted.'

He took no official action, and Leavis went on using a passage of Joyce's prose in his lectures. But the unofficial enquiries into his activities in the English school had the effect of intensifying the whispering compaign against him. More and more of his colleagues were becoming more and more determined to get rid of him. There were jokes about 'the Leavis Prize for Pornography' and, well into the thirties, long after his downfall, dons went on explaining his unpopularity by saying 'We don't like the kind of book he lends undergraduates.'

The appointment as Probationary Lecturer took effect from October 1927 and it seems to have given him confidence, at the age of thirty-two, to publish his opinions in print. In December he began to contribute occasional book reviews to *The Cambridge Review*. His first piece coupled Osbert Sitwell's *England Reclaimed* with F. R. Higgins's *The Dark Breed*. Two months later, in February 1928, he was reviewing *Critiques* by Augustus Ralli, and he wrote two more reviews before the end of the year: on George Rylands's *Words and Poetry* in June, and on Edmund Blunden's *Retreat* in October. As he said four years later in *New Bearings in English Poetry*, he rated Blunden more highly than the other Georgian poets, though less highly than Edward Thomas, who should never have been classified with them. But Leavis preferred Blunden's *The Shepherd* to his later work, such as *Retreat*. 'The visionary gleam, the vanished glory, the transcendental suggestion remain too often vague, the rhythms stumble, and the characteristic packed effects are apt to degenerate into cluttered obscurity.'

After reviewing Shane Leslie's *The Skull of Swift* for *The Cambridge Review* in January, he went on in February to write his first piece that was not a review. Titled 'T. S. Eliot – a Reply to the Condescending', it was provoked by a *New Statesman* reviewer, R. Ellis Roberts, who in December 1928 had been patronizing about *For Lancelot Andrewes – Essays on Style and Order*, describing Eliot as 'not a critic of the first trenchancy' and comparing him unfavourably with Dr Saintsbury. Leavis's negative observations about the review were only a stepping-stone to positive and extremely penetrating remarks about the relationship between Eliot the poet and Eliot the critic. 'His poetry is more conscious of the past than any other that is being written in English today. This most modern of the moderns is more truly traditional than the "traditionalists".' In *The Sacred Wood* (to which Leavis had by now returned very frequently) Eliot had written 'By losing tradition we lose our hold on the present'. As Leavis argued, John Masefield and Laurence Binyon had been limited by 'conventions of "the poetic"' which barred them from contemporary material that could have been valuable, while 'sensitive and adequate minds' were being 'barred out of poetry'.[1] As a

---

[1] The argument was not new. In 1925 Edgell Rickword had been campaigning in *The Calendar of Modern Letters* against the 'temporary social queasiness' that had

poet Eliot had transcended those limiting conventions by following the prescription he had formulated for the critic in *The Sacred Wood*: 'The important critic is the person who is absorbed in the present problems of art, and who wishes to bring the forces of the past to bear upon the solution of these problems.' Eliot became an important poet by going back to the example of Donne and Dryden. By now Eliot's verse and criticism were both exerting a strong influence both on younger poets and on critics writing about them. Preparing a course of lectures on contemporary verse, Leavis had found echoes of Eliot's *Homage to John Dryden* in current reviews and critiques.

Leavis's *Cambridge Review* article shows that he had been troubled by the question of whether it was right to devote 'a good part of our lives to the study of literature'. He had found an answer in Eliot's demonstration of 'what is meant by "an interest in art and life as problems which exist and can be handled apart from their relations to the critic's private temperament"'. The article also shows that Leavis had already found in Eliot the idea that was to germinate *Revaluation*:

> If no serious critic or poet now supposes that English poetry in the future must, or can, develop along the line running from the Romantics through Tennyson, this is mainly due to Mr Eliot.

The next book Leavis reviewed for *The Cambridge Review* was *Cambridge Poetry 1929*, which he found 'cheering, as I have found no other anthology of modern verse . . . it betokens a decisive throwing-off of the fatal conventions and preconceptions . . . Sitwellism counts for very little in it and E. E. Cummings is not there.' Dismissing J. Bronowski's poem 'October Casuistry' as parasitic and derivative, Leavis settled with unerring discrimination on William Empson and Richard Eberhart as the two poets who deserved very much more than the space allotted to them. Empson was not parasitic or derivative, though he had 'profited by the ideas that Mr Eliot has put into currency . . . It is plain that Mr Empson knows his Donne.'

By 1929, when Leavis married Queenie Dorothy Roth, the intellectual relationship between them had become symbiotic. There is clear evidence of cross-fertilization between her book *Fiction and the*

---

led to 'the erection of a literary language' in which the poet could not express 'negative emotions'.

Reading Public and her husband's pamphlet, *Mass Civilization and Minority Culture*, which came out in 1930, the first in a series called Minority Pamphlets, published by his friend Gordon Fraser at St John's College.

1930 was the year Lawrence died. The fourth pamphlet in the series consisted of two essays by John Middleton Murry, both reprinted from *The Adelphi*: 'The Poems of D. H. Lawrence' and 'The Doctrine of D. H. Lawrence', a review of *Lady Chatterley's Lover*. Before the end of the year, Leavis's 33-page pamphlet *D. H. Lawrence* appeared as the sixth in the series, propounding a view very different from the one he was later to adopt. He compared Lawrence's genius with that of Blake: they both had 'the same terrifying honesty'.[1] But 'the preoccupation with the primitive fostered in him (Lawrence) a certain inhumanity'; and Leavis was disparaging about his verse. 'Not much of it is poetry, though it is very interesting in various ways: he rarely attained the level of "Ballad of a Second Ophelia".

The thirty-five-year-old critic's assessments of the novels contrast very strikingly with his maturer value-judgments. Like *Sons and Lovers*, *The Rainbow* is criticized for bearing a close relationship with Lawrence's personal experience:

> *Sons and Lovers*, for all its poignant beauty, everyone I have discussed it with agrees with me that it is difficult to get through. *The Rainbow* is a great deal more difficult. We do not doubt the urgency for the author of these shifting tensions of the inner life, this play of the inexplicit and almost inexpressible in human intercourse, but for us the effect is one of monotony. Lawrence's fanatical concern for the 'essential' often results in a strange intensity, but how limited is the range! And the intensity too often fails to come through to us. Behind these words we know there are agonies of frustration, deadlock and apprehension, but we only see words.

Of *Women in Love* Leavis writes: 'To get through it calls for great determination and a keen diagnostic interest ... Lawrence's main interest lies much lower than personality, and the characters in *Women in Love* tend to disintegrate into swirls of conflicting impulses and emotions. It is difficult to keep them apart.' He also complains of Lawrence's mechanical use of a 'specialized vocabulary of terms that he tries to invest with a new potency by endless reiterations:

---

[1] Eliot's essay on Blake in *The Sacred Wood* refers to his 'peculiar honesty, which in a world too frightened to be honest, is peculiarly terrifying.'

"dark", "utter", "inchoate", "disintegrate", "uncreated", "violated", "abstract", "mindless", "lapse out", "loins of darkness", and so on.'

Leavis judges *The Lost Girl* to be Lawrence's 'best *novel* . . . magnificently Dickensian'. The italics prepare the way for the point that Lawrence's art is at its surest in the short stories, 'where he has no room for discursive prophecy'. *The Plumed Serpent* is dismissed as 'largely a day-dream, a wish-fulfilment'. 'It is amusing to watch him going about the world, discovering strange, strange wisdom in remote or primitive people, and suffering furious revulsion when his civilized susceptibilities are outraged. But he never fell into disillusion. His splendid genius burnt always with a fierce flame.'

Basic to the conception of Q. D. Leavis's *Fiction and the Reading Public* is a notion about the relationship between the present and the past which obviously derives from T. S. Eliot, while the method used for the 'anthropological' investigation of the contemporary situation may have been inspired by I. A. Richards's technique with his protocols. To discover more about popular novelists and popular reading habits she sent out a questionnaire to sixty authors, twenty-five of whom sent back useful answers. She classified seventeen of these twenty-five as 'absolute best-sellers', one as 'highbrow' and seven as middlebrow, sub-dividing these into four who were read as 'literature' and three who were not. The questionnaire asked them to explain their popularity and to compare it with that of their nineteenth-century predecessors, including Scott and Dickens. They were invited to give their views on the best-seller, to analyse the factors that influenced its circulation, to tell the story of how they turned to fiction as a profession, to describe the whole process of creating a novel, from conception to commercial promotion, and to give the gist of letters received from admiring readers. One of the most articulate and intelligent replies came from Edgar Rice Burroughs, creator of *Tarzan*, who compared his fiction with cinema:

> It has been discovered through repeated experiments that pictures that require thought for appreciation have invariably been box-office failures. The general public does not wish to think. This fact, probably more than any other, accounts for the success of my stories, for without this specific idea in mind I have, nevertheless, endeavoured to make all of my descriptions so clear that each situation could be visualized readily

by any reader precisely as I saw it. My reason for doing this was not based upon a low estimate of general intelligence, but upon the realization that in improbable situations, such as abound in my work, the greatest pains must be taken to make them appear plausible. I have evolved, therefore, a type of fiction that may be read with the minimum of mental effort.

This is quoted in *Fiction and the Reading Public* with the penultimate sentence omitted and (without the omission) in a footnote to *Mass Civilization and Minority Culture* with an acknowledgment about being privileged to see the letter.

Both the pamphlet and the book are primarily concerned with the debasement of standards since the Shakespearean period, as popular fiction and journalism reduced their demands on the public's ability to think. Leavis wrote:

Hamlet appealed at a number of levels of response, from the highest downwards. The same is true of *Paradise Lost, Clarissa, Tom Jones, Don Juan, The Return of the Native.* The same is not true . . . of *The Waste Land, Hugh Selwyn Mauberley, Ulysses* or *To the Lighthouse.* These works are read only by a very small specialized public and are beyond the reach of the vast majority of those who consider themselves educated. The age in which the finest creative talent tends to be employed in works of this kind is the age that has given currency to the term 'high-brow'. But it would be as true to say that the attitude implicit in 'high-brow' causes this use of talent as the converse.

He had made the point earlier that:

The minority capable not only of appreciating Dante, Shakespeare, Donne, Baudelaire, Hardy (to take major instances) but of recognizing their latest successors constitute the consciousness of the race (or of a branch of it) at a given time . . . Upon this minority depends our power of profiting by the finest human experience of the past; they keep alive the subtlest and most perishable parts of tradition. Upon them depend the implicit standards that order the finer living of an age, the sense that this is worth more than that, this rather than that is the direction in which to go, that the centre is here rather than there. In their keeping . . . is the language, the changing idiom, upon which fine living depends, and without which distinction of spirit is thwarted and incoherent. By 'culture' I mean the use of such a language.

He went on to analyse the process of cultural 'levelling-down' that accompanied 'the processes of mass-production and standardization in the form represented by the Press'. While Lord Northcliffe 'showed

people what they wanted, and showed the Best People that they
wanted the same as the rest', films involved 'surrender, under conditions of hypnotic receptivity, to the cheapest emotional appeals,
appeals the more insidious because they are associated with a com-
pellingly vivid illusion of actual life.' Broadcasting was 'in practice
mainly a means of passive diversion', which tended 'to make active
recreation, especially active use of the mind, more difficult'. Meanwhile advertising was 'doing a great deal for English. It is carrying
on the work begun by Mr Rudyard Kipling, and, where certain
important parts of the vocabulary are concerned, making things
more difficult for the fastidious.' In his influential book column in the
Evening Standard Arnold Bennett was scoffing at *The Waste Land* and
Virginia Woolf, and enthusing about *Jew Süss, The Bridge of San Luis
Rey*, Edith Sitwell, the novels of R. H. Mottram and *Vivandière* by
Phoebe Fenwick Gaye, while The Book Society and The Book Guild
were emulating the success achieved in America by the Book of the
Month Club.

Fiction and the Reading Public deploys its carefully researched
material to reinforce the point about cultural decline. 'The closer
one looks the more fully one is persuaded that the life of the people
at the end of the seventeenth century and of the shopkeeper class at
the beginning of the eighteenth century was in general both finer in
quality and more satisfying in substance than that of their descen-
dants whose reading habits have been described in Part 1.' Mrs
Leavis makes the same complaint about the Book Society's cham-
pionship of second-rate literature and she quotes the same cutting
from the *Evening Standard* to show that the first edition of *Vivandière*
was sold out as a result of Arnold Bennett's encomium.

Many of her value-judgments on English fiction were later to be
endorsed by her husband. Two of his essays echo her admiration for
The Pilgrim's Progress and her insistence that the Puritan culture
deserves as much credit as John Bunyan for producing it. The
exclusion of Fielding and Smollett from Leavis's 1948 book *The Great
Tradition* is illuminated by a sentence among the notes at the end of
Fiction and the Reading Public:

> If one examines Fielding and Smollett with Bunyan in mind, it becomes
> evident that their principal characters are simply-perceived types
> drawn from outside in the tradition of the Theophrastian character-
> writing, and the minor roles filled up with variations on the conven-
> tional humorous and eccentric characters of the contemporary drama.

Except for a chapter on *Hard Times*, Dickens is also excluded from *The Great Tradition*. Both Leavises were later to change their minds about his importance and his artistry, collaborating on *Dickens the Novelist*, which appeared in 1970, but *Fiction and the Reading Public* dismisses him as 'the Victorian equivalent of Defoe':

> Whereas Sterne's successors at any rate represent a cultivation of the emotions founded on a gentle code, Dickens stands primarily for a set of crude emotional exercises. He discovered, for instance, the formula 'laughter and tears' that has been the foundation of practically every popular success ever since (Hollywood's as well as the bestsellers) . . . The peculiarity of Dickens . . . is that his originiality is confined to recapturing a child's outlook on the grown-up world, emotionally he is not only uneducated but also immature.

T. S. Eliot, who liked *Mass Civilization and Minority Culture*, invited Leavis to write a pamphlet for the 'Criterion Miscellany'. Accepting the commission, he wrote an essay on the current state of criticism, but after a long silence, the news came that Eliot would prefer not to publish it. The substance of it appeared later, in September 1932, in the second issue of *Scrutiny* under the title 'What's Wrong with Criticism?' Leavis developed the argument he had started in *Mass Civilization and Minority Culture*, using recent books of criticism by H. W. Garrod, Bonamy Dobrée and Desmond MacCarthy to demonstrate that the function of criticism had fallen into abeyance:

> To those who take a serious interest in literature it must often seem as if their interest were curiously irrelevant to the modern world; curiously, because a serious interest in literature starts from the present and assumes that literature matters, in the first place at any rate, as the consciousness of the age. If a literary tradition does not keep itself alive here, in the present, not merely in new creation, but as a pervasive influence upon feeling, thought and standards of living (it is time we challenged the economist's use of this phrase), then it must be pronounced to be dying or dead. Indeed, it seems hardly likely that, when this kind of influence becomes negligible, creation will long persist. In any case, a consciousness maintained by an insulated minority and without effect upon the powers that rule the world has lost its function.

This article might have started a useful controversy if it had appeared either in the 'Criterion Miscellany' series, or in *The Criterion*, but it was too outspoken for Eliot, though probably he would not have disagreed with the ending of Leavis's article, which applied a quotation from Matthew Arnold to the current situation:

> It is not that there do not exist in England, as in France, a number of people perfectly well able to discern what is good, in these things, from what is bad; but they are isolated, they form no powerful body of opinion, they are not strong enough to set a standard . . . Ignorance and charlatanism . . . are always trying to pass off their wares as excellent, and to cry down criticism as the voice of an insignificant, over-fastidious minority.

But Eliot remained unsympathetic to both Leavis and *Scrutiny*. William Empson remembers going to his office at Faber and Faber 'to ask for a book to review for the *Criterion*, and he was looking at the current *Scrutiny* while talking about it to someone else; how disgusting the behaviour of Leavis was, what mob oratory his arguments were, couldn't something be done to stop him? – and then, with cold indignation, "Of course, I know it's going to be me next."'

Of all the literary reviews before *Scrutiny*, it was *The Calendar of Modern Letters* that had made the most intelligent attempt to raise critical standards, to rally the discerning minority and to give it a platform. It was much livelier than *The Criterion*, but it lasted only from March 1925 to July 1927, publishing twelve monthly and then six quarterly issues.[1] *Scrutiny*, which took its name from the series of critical evaluations, 'Scrutinies', that had appeared in *The Calendar*, paid generous tribute to it in the opening Manifesto, but it did not aim to continue from where *The Calendar* had left off. Its failure proved that even with prices as low as they had been in the twenties, high quality could not guarantee a sufficient income from subscriptions, casual sales and advertisements to pay contributors and cover production costs. One advantage of being based in Cambridge was that it would be easier to find contributors who did not expect to be paid.

The Probationary Lectureships could be held for a maximum of four years, but in 1928, when three University Lectureships fell vacant, Enid Welsford, T. R. Henn and L. J. Potts were promoted. Together with Joan Bennett and Basil Willey, Leavis stayed on as a probationary lecturer until 1931. Basil Willey was the first of the three to be offered a permanent position, but he had to wait until 1934. When another lectureship fell vacant, in 1935, an outsider,

[1] I have discussed *The Calendar* at length in *The New Review* I 12, March 1975.

George Rylands, was given precedence over both Leavis and Joan Bennett. He had to wait until 1936 and she until 1937.[1]

Possibly 'Q' could have done more than he did to help Leavis, but at least he did not take part in the movement to find a job for him as far away from Cambridge as possible. He was advised to accept a position in Tasmania, but he had no intention of leaving Cambridge, even if he had to stay on without a job. The undergraduates he wanted to teach were there, not in the southern hemisphere. His determination to stay caused considerable embarrassment and considerable hardship. Thanks to Hilda Murray, he was able to earn some money from taking supervisions at Girton. He taught there for three hours every Wednesday afternoon in an old army hut with a tin roof. He would be seen putting a tie on outside the college and stuffing it back into his pocket at the beginning of his cycle ride.

There is a story that one day while cycling to Girton he made up a sonnet out of phrases taken from other poems. When he wrote it up on a blackboard the girls thought it was a masterpiece and, not wanting to divulge its authorship, he had great difficulty in convincing them that it was a bogus piece of work.

The instinct that made Leavis defy all the indications that he was unwanted in Cambridge told him there was something constructive to be done which could be done nowhere else. The story of his life between 1927 and 1932 could be told as if the idea of a new magazine were central to his motivations. It would be unfair to suggest that he and Mrs Leavis started their Friday tea-parties with the idea of collecting potential contributors. But the atmosphere in their large house in Chesterton Hall Crescent was pleasant, their hospitality was generous, Queenie Leavis's home-made cakes and scones were delicious and the tea-parties were soon attracting many of the most interesting people in Cambridge, including Wittgenstein. If the house became an unofficial centre of 'Cambridge English', it was because

---

[1] I am indebted here to Noël Annan and his letter of 12 December 1975 in the *Times Literary Supplement*. Between 5 December 1975 and 9 January 1976, letters were appearing in its correspondence column from Dr Leavis, Lord Annan, Henri Fluchère and me, all arising out of the *Commentary* in the *Times Literary Supplement* of 28 November about my essay on Leavis in *The New Review* II 19, November 1975. Background information about the beginnings of the English Faculty at Cambridge is also to be found in two memoirs: E. M. W. Tillyard's *The Muse Unchained: an Intimate Account of the Revolution in English Studies*, London 1958, and Basil Willey's *Cambridge and Other Memoirs 1920–1953*, London 1968.

the hosts and so many of their guests cared about literature and the opportunities that were being wasted in the way it was being taught. As Leavis said later, it was these Friday tea-parties that made it possible for *Scrutiny* to be launched successfully.

To understand Leavis is to understand that his decisions are taken without giving himself any freedom of choice, and his personal courage has usually enabled him to obey the commands of his conscience. His friendship with Wittgenstein was initiated by the categorical imperative that prompted him to pursue the philosopher out of a tea-party in order to tell him off for behaving so badly. They met in 1929 at the house of W. H. Johnson, the logician who had supervised all the Cambridge philosophers from Bertrand Russell onwards. Johnson and his sister, Miss Fanny, were 'at home' on Sunday afternoons to Moral Sciences lecturers, old pupils and visiting philosophers, rather in the way that Leavis was 'at home' on Fridays. There was a grand piano in their drawing-room, and at one tea-party a young viscount was asked to sing some Schubert. Standing up, he glanced nervously across the room at a face Leavis describes as 'beautiful and stern':

'Er, Wittgenstein will correct my German.'

'How can I?' retorted Wittgenstein crushingly. 'How can I possibly?'

This effectively undermined the viscount's performance, and as soon as it was over, Wittgenstein left triumphantly. Or so it seemed to Leavis, who was angry enough to pursue him out of the crowded drawing-room. He caught up with him in the Barton Road.

'You behaved in a disgraceful way to that young man.'

'I thought he was a very foolish young man.'

'You may have done, you may have done, but you have no right to treat him like that. You have no right to treat anyone like that.'

Wittgenstein then surprised Leavis by putting a hand on his shoulder. 'We must know one another.'

Leavis muttered 'I don't see the necessity,' and strode off towards the Grantchester footpath. Soon afterwards Wittgenstein appeared at the Leavises' house and, during the next few years, often came to their tea-parties.[1]

[1] F. R. Leavis, 'Memories of Wittgenstein' in *The Human World* No. 10, February 1973.

3   *New Bearings in English Poetry* and *How to Teach Reading*

1932 was the *annus mirabilis* in the lives of the Leavises. When the first *Scrutiny* appeared in May, *Fiction and the Reading Public* and *New Bearings in English Poetry* were already on sale in the bookshops, and at the beginning of the new academic year, in October, though still not employed by the university, Leavis was taken on by one of the colleges, Downing, to succeed A. J. Wyatt as Director of Studies in English. W. L. Cuttle, who had been at Emmanuel with Leavis, had persuaded the college authorities that he was a man who could raise the level of English teaching. The appointment turned out to be an excellent long-term investment, increasing the college's prestige, attracting a great many American students to it, and winning it a spectacular proportion of Firsts in the English Tripos.

In the twenties, when Leavis had first had his vision of an alternative Cambridge, he had not been able to take any action towards bringing it into existence. But marriage, publication and employment had increased his confidence, and, with it, his strength. James Smith, who had been in America and returned to England in time to review a book for the second issue of *Scrutiny*, noticed a big difference in the impression Leavis made.

He was now thirty-seven. Besides working at Girton, he had been supervising some students from Christ's, but it was at Downing that he now had his first opportunity to take full responsibility for a group of students. The freshmen due to start reading English in October received lists of recommended books, including *Fiction and the Reading Public* and *New Bearings in English Poetry*. Arriving in Cambridge, they had their first meeting with him in a drab little classroom. He came in wearing a dirty mackintosh over an open-necked shirt, with a copy of the *New Statesman* under his arm, and as soon as he started talking he gave them the impression of being a man who could provide real help – an impression which intensified over the subsequent weeks. He did not think they would get very much from most of the lecturers but they should try for themselves and decide which ones were worthwhile.

He was cynical about the value of examinations but realistic about the strategy of preparing for them, offering shrewd hints on how questions should be tackled. He weighed in with Dryden to mop up any Romantic prejudices that sixth-form English masters might have left with them, and he spent a lot of time on Practical Criticism, comparing one passage of verse or prose with another. His intention was to give them every possible opportunity to think for themselves and to argue back; probably he underestimated the weight of his own cogency in the teaching situation. Many of them felt what students were to go on feeling throughout his career: that it was difficult to listen critically or agree selectively. The tendency was to accept everything *in toto*.

It is possible that he would have talked at them less and with them more if he had also been working as a lecturer. Supervisions still had to provide the only outlet for the teaching impulse that had been confined for years to a narrow trickle, and students later discovered that they had been listening to ideas that were developed in *Scrutiny* articles and in his 1936 book *Revaluation: Tradition and Development in English Poetry*. By the time he began lecturing again, he had habituated himself to un-Socratic dominance of tutorial conversations. According to a later pupil, 'The best supervisions were the dating classes, where we were expected to say something, and this tended to set him off at unexpected tangents. The dating classes also brought out how extraordinarily wide his reading was and how many unexpected people he seemed able to characterize in an appreciative way. I'm almost certain they included Hopkins's Canon Dixon.'

During 1931, the year of his thirty-sixth birthday, Leavis had published nothing except the two Minority Pamphlets, a review of Empson's *Seven Types of Ambiguity* in *The Cambridge Review*, an article on 'The Influence of Donne on Modern Poetry' in *The Bookman* and a review for it grouping critical books by Empson, Edmund Wilson, Wilson Knight, Herbert Read and Middleton Murry together with *Scrutinies II*, a collection of critical essays in the manner of *The Calendar*, edited by Edgell Rickword. But between 1932 and 1934, in addition to *New Bearings* and a spate of articles in *Scrutiny*, book reviews and letters to the press, Leavis published *How to Teach Reading: a Primer for Ezra Pound*, a 49-page pamphlet; *For Continuity*, which collected most of his contributions to the first six issues of *Scrutiny*; *Culture and Environment: The Training of Critical Awareness*, a textbook written in collaboration with Denys Thompson; *Towards Standards of Criticism*, a selection from *The Calendar*; and *Determinations*, a selection of *Scrutiny* essays by ten writers. Leavis edited these two books with an Introduction. His students at Downing had the excited impression of being close to the epicentre of a stormy movement that could become important, judging from the hostility it was provoking. Some of the Cambridge bookshops were refusing to stock *Scrutiny*. Storm Jameson had been the only influential reviewer to treat *Fiction and the Reading Public* respectfully: the others had either ignored it or savaged it. No review of *New Bearings* appeared in *The Criterion*, the *New Statesman* or even in *The Cambridge Review*. As Leavis wrote in 1963:

> Cambridge . . . figured for us civilization's anti-Marxist recognition of its own nature and needs . . . It was our strength to be, in our consciousness of our effort, and actually, in the paradoxical and ironical way I have to record, representatives of that Cambridge. We were, in fact, that Cambridge; we felt it, and had more and more reason to feel it, and our confidence and courage came from that. In the strength of the essential Cambridge which it consciously and explicitly represented, *Scrutiny* not only survived the hostility of the institutional academic powers; it became – who now questions it? – the clear triumphant justification of the world of Cambridge as a humane centre. In Cambridge it was the vitalizing force that gave the English school its reputation and influence, and its readers in the world at large, small as the subscribing public was, formed an incomparably influential community.

The threat to conservative complacency was all the greater because the new movement was not merely literary. It was cultural and educational; it was also anti-Marxist. *New Bearings* describes the poet as being 'at the most conscious point of the race in his time'. Similarly, *Fiction and the Reading Public* and *Culture and Environment* both make the point that literature can be an expression of communal consciousness. Both books demonstrate that Bunyan, D. H. Lawrence and George Sturt, the author of *Change in the Village* and *The Wheelwright's Shop*, used words in a way that depended on the continuing existence of an organic community which was still thriving in Bunyan's day, disappearing in Sturt's and vestigial in Lawrence's. Proceeding

along lines laid down by Matthew Arnold and I. A. Richards,
Culture and Environment argues that

> It is on literary tradition that the office of maintaining continuity must
> rest . . . What we have lost is the organic community with the living
> culture it embodied. Folk-songs, folk-dances, Cotswold cottages and
> handicraft products are signs and expressions of something more: an art
> of life, a way of living, ordered and patterned, involving social arts,
> codes of intercourse and a responsive adjustment, growing out of im-
> memorial experience, to the natural environment and the rhythm of the
> year . . . The machine has destroyed the old ways of life, the old forms,
> and by reason of the continuous rapid change it involves, prevented the
> growth of new.

Denys Thompson was now Senior English Master at Gresham's
School, Holt. He had been taught by Leavis and found him 'very
kind, tolerant of youthful brashness' and able to provide 'a start and
impetus that lasted'. Thompson has said that his part in *Culture and
Environment* was to advise on school conditions and possibilities; that
the book was essentially Leavis's in conception and method. Leavis,
whose energy at this time must have been prodigious, has said that
it was written in a week.

It wielded a tremendous influence, penetrating into classrooms
and encouraging sixth-formers to examine their environment as
critically as they were learning to examine literature. 'A modern
education worthy of the name must be largely an education against
the environment . . . The aim of education should be to give command of the art of living.' *Culture and Environment* consists of examples,
questions and exercises, but the titles of the sections show that the
book has roots in the same incisive connubial thinking that had gone
into *Fiction and the Reading Public*: 'Advertising: Types of Appeal;
The Place of Advertising in a Modern Economy; Mass-Production;
Standardisation; Levelling-Down; The Supply of Reading Matter;
Advertising, Fiction and the Currency of National Life; Progress
and the Standard of Living; The Use of Leisure; Tradition; The
Organic Community; The Loss of the Organic Community; Substitute Living; Education.'

The concept of the 'organic community' has been challenged by
Raymond Williams, who dismisses it as a myth, attacking Leavis for
his acceptance of George Eliot's social values and Sturt for his
'conventionally foreshortened version of history'. In a lecture printed

in *Nor Shall My Sword* Leavis defends the concept and the use they had made of it to clarify the human problems caused by the 'accelerating technological revolution':

> The wheelwright's business . . . didn't merely provide him with a satisfying craft that entailed the use of a diversity of skills; it contained a full meaning in itself – it kept a human significance always present, and this was a climate in which the craftsman lived and worked: lived as he worked. Its materials were for the most part locally grown, and the wheelwright quite commonly had noted as a tree in situ the timber that came to the shop – which is a representative aspect of the general truth. The customers too were local, and he knew them, themselves and their settings, as meeting their particular requirements he had to, individually – he, the wheelwright of the neighbourhood. He saw the products of his craft in use, serving their functions in the life and purpose of a community that really was a community, a human microcosm, and couldn't help feeling itself one.

The essay by which Leavis represented himself in *Determinations* was 'The Irony of Swift', which suggests that his essential qualities are not most evident in *Gulliver's Travels*, where the main satisfaction for the adult reader is in the ironic seasoning 'which Swift, the student of the *Mariner's Magazine* and of travellers' relations, aimed to supply in the bare precision and the matter-of-fact realness of his narrative'. More important is 'a peculiar emotional intensity', which is evident in the account of the Struldbrugs and the Yahoos, but more evident in other works. It is mainly destructive even when he is eager to use it as a weapon of defence – in *The Argument Against Abolishing Christianity*, for instance. Where Gibbon's irony implies a solidarity with the reader, 'the implied solidarity in Swift is itself ironical – a means to betrayal'. The irony 'is essentially a matter of surprise and negation; its function is to defeat habit, to intimidate and to demoralize. What he assumes in the *Argument* is not so much a common acceptance of Christianity as that the reader will be ashamed to have to recognize how fundamentally unchristian his actual assumptions, motives, and attitudes are. And in general the implication is that it would shame people if they were made to recognize themselves unequivocally.'

As Dr Johnson observed, Swift's powers are given full play in *The Tale of a Tub*. What Johnson called 'copiousness of images' derives

from something that can be seen both 'in the sardonic vivacity of
comic vision that characterizes the narrative' and 'in the spontaneous metaphorical energy of Swift's prose – in the image, action
or blow that, leaping out of the prosaic manner, continually sur-
prises and disconcerts the reader'. In Swift's use of negative emotions
and attitudes 'there is something that it is difficult not to call creative,
though the aim always is destructive.' The most damage is inflicted
when the most energy is generated out of the tension between impulse
of appeal (in the argument) and revulsion (in the emotion). Leavis
reinforces his analysis with practical criticism, quoting at length
from the *Digression Concerning the Origin, the Use, and Improvement of
Madness in a Commonwealth* and interpolating his commentary. He
concludes that in Swift we have 'probably the most remarkable
expression of negative feelings and attitudes that literature can
offer'.

It was characteristic of Leavis that in dedicating *New Bearings* to his
dead father and his wife, he designated both by their initials. In the
Prefatory Note he paid tribute to *The Calendar*, 'that uniquely intelligent review which, from 1925 to 1927, was, it is hardly excessive to
say, the critical consciousness of the younger adult generations'. The
phrasing of this sentence pinpoints his own ambition: his own books
and the criticism he published in *Scrutiny* should (in both senses of
the word) inform the critical consciousness of the new generation.
    'Poetry and the Modern World' is the title of his first chapter,
which attacks 'the great bulk of the verse that is culled and offered
to us as the fine flower of modern poetry . . . The words that lie there
arranged on the page have no roots: the writer himself can never
have been more than superficially interested in them.' As in his
article on Eliot for *The Cambridge Review*, he argued that in any
period the prevalent habits, conventions and preconceptions affect
the ways poets use their talent. The preconceptions about 'the
poetical' that still dominated the early thirties had been established
in the period of the great Romantics. They had been formulated in
the previous century by Joseph Warton, when he wrote (apropos of
Pope) that the 'sublime and the pathetic are the two chief nerves of
all genuine poesy.' 'Our only three sublime and pathetic poets' were
Spenser, Shakespeare and Milton. Unlike the Romantics, who
believed 'that the interests animating their poetry were the forces

moving the world', the Victorian poets had assumed 'that the actual world is alien, recalcitrant and unpoetical, and that no protest is worth making except the protest of withdrawal'.

Yeats said that he learned to think when Pre-Raphaelitism was in the middle of its final phase. 'Only ancient things and the stuff of dreams were beautiful'.[1] Leavis illustrates the dependence of his early verse on Keats, Tennyson and William Morris. In *The Wind among the Reeds* (1899) Yeats was channelling both exaltation and despair into the dream-world which served him as a substitute for the hateful quotidian actuality presented by the scientists, the naturalistic novelists and the playwrights, like Ibsen, who served up 'dialogue so close to modern educated speech that music and style were impossible'.[2] But Yeats was capable of developing beyond this phase. He saw that 'The dream-world of Morris was as much the antithesis of daily life as with other men of genius, but he was never conscious of the antithesis and so knew nothing of intellectual suffering.' Yeats's own awareness of the antithesis heightened his intellectual suffering, helping him towards the mature achievement of *The Green Helmet* (1912). As Leavis comments, 'The verse, in its rhythm and diction, recognizes the actual world, but holds against it an ideal of aristocratic fineness. . . . To pass from the earlier verse to this is something like passing from Campion to Donne.' But Yeats's development was less fruitful than it might have been 'if the poetic tradition of the nineteenth century had been less completely unlike the Metaphysical tradition . . . *The Tower* (1928) merely develops the manner of *The Green Helmet* (1912), *Responsibilities* (1914) and *The Wild Swans at Coole* (1919).'

After devoting 24 pages to Yeats, Leavis spends six on Walter de la Mare: 'To be able to work so insidious a spell as successfully as he does in his best poetry is to be in some measure a victim of it oneself.' Hardy receives only the same amount of space, though 'He inhabits a solid world, with the earth firm under his feet.' Leavis give us an excellent commentary on his 1912 poem 'The Voice', but concludes that 'his rank as a major poet rests upon a dozen poems. These are lost among a vast bulk of verse interesting only by its oddity and idiosyncrasy, and as illustrating the habits that somehow become strength in his great poetry.' This seems unfair. I am more inclined to agree with Thom Gunn: 'If the price paid for his fifty

[1] *Autobiographies*, p. 101.
[2] Ibid, p. 343.

best poems is some hundreds of bad ones, it is well paid.' But then
Leavis obviously thinks 'the lilt of popular airs' damaging to Hardy,
while Thom Gunn welcomes the convergence of the ballad tradition
with that of the reflective lyric in Hardy's work.[1]

More than a quarter of the book is occupied by a brilliant chapter
on Eliot. Leavis argues that in the 1917 collection 'Prufrock' is
inferior to 'Portrait of a Lady', which is more subtly poised, the
idiom of modern speech going perfectly with the movement of the
verse. Laforgue and Corbière suggested starting points unlike any
that could have been found in nineteenth-century English literature.
The ironical transitions and the self-distrustful attitudes are derived
largely from Laforgue, but to learn from verse in a language so unlike English in its movement, a poet must be strongly original.
Already 'he is himself as only a major poet can be'. Similarly Leavis,
in spite of his dependence on everything Eliot's poetry and criticism
had done to change the tradition, is by now himself as only a major
critic can be.

He settles on *Gerontion* (which was published in the 1920 volume)
as the outstanding early Eliot poem; nowhere outside Shakespeare
'can we find a passage so sustained in quality'. Leavis's discussion
of it prefigures *Revaluation* in its critical procedure. Keats's first
Hyperion points backwards to Milton and forwards to Tennyson;
Eliot restores to English poetry conversational qualities which had
been absent from it since the Jacobeans. Gerard Manley Hopkins,
the only Victorian poet capable of reinstating these qualities, had
himself been kept out of the picture. When other nineteenth-century
poets tried to imitate Shakespeare, the influence was filtered damag-
ingly through Milton. 'There is no pressure in his verse of any
complex and varying current of feeling and sensation; the words
have little substance or muscular quality: Milton is using only a
small part of the resources of the English language. . . . A man's
most vivid emotional and sensuous experience is inevitably bound
up with the language that he actually speaks,' but Milton's poetic
idiom is remote from his everyday speech.

Leavis describes *The Waste Land* (1922) as 'an effort to focus an
inclusive human consciousness'. Banality is reproduced with an
undertone that creates resonance. The religious element makes its
first appearance in the final section, 'What the Thunder Said'. The

---

[1] 'Hardy and the Ballads' in *Agenda* Vol. 10, Nos. 2–3, Spring–Summer 1972.

Hanged Man on the Tarot card is equated with Christ and with the Vegetation God, while the journey through the Waste Land becomes the Journey to Emmaus. The recurrent quotations and literary allusions are justified because they help Eliot to a compression that could not have been obtained in any other way – 'the co-presence in the mind of a number of different orientations, fundamental attitudes, orders of experience.'

The three Ariel Poems of 1927–9 receive short shrift. The 'fevered torment' of *The Hollow Men* (1925) has given way to 'inert resignation. The movements are tired and nerveless.' The rhythms of *Ash-Wednesday* (1930) have far more life. In his essay on Dante (1929), Eliot characterized his visual imagination as belonging to an age in which men had visions. It was 'a psychological habit' which 'was once a more significant, interesting, and disciplined kind of dreaming.' Leavis illuminatingly applies this point to 'the dreamcrossed twilight' of *Ash-Wednesday*. In the fourth poem syntax and structure are used to create ambiguity which expresses doubt; in the final poem 'the doubt becomes an adjuvant of spiritual discipline, ministering to humility.' But the inescapable ambiguity remains. The religious poetry 'may lack the charged richness and the range of *Gerontion* and *The Waste Land*. But it is, perhaps, still more remarkable by reason of the strange and difficult regions of experience that it explores . . . and the devotion to spiritual discipline should not hinder the reader from seeing that the modes of feeling, apprehension and expression are such as we can find nowhere earlier.'

Writing in 1931, Leavis could not have known how much *The Waste Land* had benefited from Ezra Pound's stringent, quasi-editorial cutting. Not that the knowledge would have altered Leavis's valuation of Pound's poetry, though it might have helped him to understand why Eliot regarded his friend as the better wordsmith. The more in sympathy with a writer a critic is, the better he can deal with him; temperamentally Leavis was as much at odds with Pound as he was in tune with Eliot. Leavis focused his whole life on the town he was born in; Eliot tore up his New England roots to plant himself deliberately in this England; in exiling himself from America, Pound committed himself more to Europe than to England. This not only had profound effects on his use of the English language, it helps to explain his attitude to translation, his use of foreign languages and his avoidance of the Shakespearean tradition.

Discussing *The Waste Land*, Leavis had objected that the irony 'of the *Shantih shantih shantih* that ends the poem is largely ineffective, for Mr Eliot's note that " 'The Peace which passeth understanding' is a feeble translation of the content of this word" can impart to the word only a feeble ghost of that content for the Western reader.' Pound's work bristles with foreign phrases unexplained by notes. The Chinese is always irritating, but with other languages the suggestiveness of the sounds sometimes compensates for our failure to pick up nuances of meaning, as I think it does with Eliot's 'Shantih'. This line of defence would not have been acceptable to Leavis, whose chapter on Pound is the one unsatisfactory chapter in the book. There is only one poem to which he responds positively enough to provide a valuable commentary — *Hugh Selwyn Mauberley*, Pound's highly sophisticated, highly ironical view of a poet's experience in London, perspectived by literary traditions, novelistic and epic. Even here, Leavis misses some of the irony, calling the poem 'quintessential autobiography'. In fact there is usually a degree of critical separation between Pound and his persona, though this varies from section to section.[1]

Though it is slightly misleading to suggest that 'What we have in *Mauberley* is a representative sensibility, that of a poet who found his starting point in the 'nineties', Leavis is right to stress the influence of Swinburne, Yeats and William Morris on Pound's early work. But, like Eliot,[2] Leavis ignores the influence of Walt Whitman, while emphasizing the dependence of Pound's versification on his English predecessors. Leavis is also at fault in calling Pound an aesthete. His poetry, says Leavis, lacks 'Mr Eliot's complex intensities of concern about soul and body: the moral, religious and anthropological preoccupations are absent.' I would have said that the preoccupations were as much moral as aesthetic.

The less at home he is with a writer, the more Leavis tends to peer over the shoulders of other critics, and most of his mistakes about Pound result from failing to push Eliot out of the way. Eliot's Introduction contains the sentence

> I confess that I am seldom interested in what he is saying, but only in the way he says it.

---

[1] For those who don't want to read a whole book on *Mauberley* the best approach is to take Leavis's chapter in conjunction with the chapters in Hugh Kenner's *The Poetry of Ezra Pound* (Faber 1951) Donald Davie's *Ezra Pound: Poet as Sculptor* (Routledge 1964) and Davie's *Pound* (Fontana 1975).

[2] In his Introduction to Pound's *Selected Poems*. Faber 1928.

Leavis's comment is:

> It seems improbable that a way of saying that can be so sharply distinguished from the thing said could do much towards re-orientating English poetry.

This is taking it for granted that the distinction is valid. Instead of questioning this, Leavis questions 'the quality of Mr Pound's own interest in what he says. His various addictions – Provençal, Italian, Chinese – speak the amateur.' Later on, Leavis quite rightly challenges Eliot's separation of 'philosophy' from style in Pound's *Cantos*. If the separation were valid, it would have 'limited very drastically the kind of importance that can be attributed to the *Cantos*,' but Leavis seems less interested in coming to grips with Pound's text than in the incompatibility of Eliot's separation with the implicit claim he made for the *Cantos*: 'they are the only "poem of some length" by any of my contemporaries that I can read with enjoyment and admiration.' In the Retrospect he wrote for the 1950 edition of *New Bearings*, Leavis is much more outspoken in his dismissal of the *Cantos*: 'how boring that famous versification actually is – boring with the emptiness of the egotism it thrusts on us. A poet's creativity can hardly be a matter of mere versification; there is no profound creative impulse at all for Pound's technical skill to serve ... His versification and his *procédés* are servants of wilful ideas and platform vehemences. His moral attitudes and absolutisms are bullying assertions, and have the uncreative blatancy of one whose Social Credit consorts naturally with Fascism and Anti-Semitism.' Twenty years later[1] Leavis wrote to *The Times Literary Supplement* quoting a letter that Eliot, 'towards the very end of his life' had written to him:

> I agree with you about Pound & the aridity of the *Cantos*, with the exception of at least one item & a few lines from one of the so-called Pisan *Cantas* where it seems to me also that a touch of humanity breaks through; I mean the lovely verse of 'Bow (sic) down thy vanity' and the reference to the negro who knocked him up a table when he was in the cafe at Pisa. And of course Pound's incomparable sense of rhythm carries a lot over. But I do find the *Cantos*, apart from that exceptional moment, quite arid and depressing.

Possibly the Cantos would have added up to more if there were less of them or if Pound had invited Eliot to edit them as he edited *The Waste Land*, but I would argue that it is as unreasonable to reject the

[1] 11 September 1970.

whole work as it would be to reject the whole of Hardy's poetry on the grounds that only twelve poems are entirely successful. I think Donald Davie is throwing out the right hint about the Cantos when he says we should 'read many at a time, and fast'. The first eight Cantos arguably exercised a stronger influence than *Mauberley* on Eliot's work, while Canto LXXXI represents one of the pinnacles of modern poetic achievement.

Leavis's chapter on Gerard Manley Hopkins is incomparably better. To describe him as 'the only influential poet of the Victorian age' is to ignore Browning's influence on Pound, but Leavis substantiates his contention that Hopkins 'was one of the most remarkable technical inventors who ever wrote, and he was a major poet'. The first collected edition of his verse had belatedly been published in 1918, and, eight years later, I. A. Richards had written what was probably 'the first intelligent critique' in *The Dial*. In 1930 it had still been possible for Thomas Sturge Moore to think he could improve on Hopkins by rewriting 'The Leaden Echo and the Golden Echo', ironing out the metrical irregularities and discarding 'his most ludicrous redundancies'. T. S. Eliot published Sturge Moore's 'Style and Beauty in Literature', which included the rewrite, in *The Criterion*.[1]

Leavis demonstrates that Hopkins used his unorthodox devices to express complexities of feeling and to catch movements of consciousness. In spite of the strains, the clogging and the defiance of grammatical rules, Hopkins was bringing poetry closer to living speech. He was also profiting like no other Victorian from the Shakespearean example. One of Leavis's most instructive comparisons is between Macbeth's 'cabin'd, cribb'd, confined' and Hopkins's use of alliteration, assonance and accumulation of verbal stress to generate emotional intensities, at the same time concentrating a maximum of the reader's attention on each word:

> How a lush-kept plush-capped
> sloe
> Will, mouthed to flesh-burst,
> Gush! – flush the man, the being with it, sour or sweet,
> Brim, in a flash, full!

Leavis also cites Empson's *Seven Types of Ambiguity* to refute Robert Bridges's silly argument that 'ambiguity or momentary uncertainty destroys the force of the sentence'.

[1] July 1930.

Leavis's Epilogue argues that Eliot, Pound and Hopkins 'together represent a decisive re-ordering of the tradition of English poetry'. The achievement of *New Bearings* was one of consolidation. As George Steiner pointed out in 1962,[1] 'Eliot, Ezra Pound and Robert Graves had already proclaimed the quality of the new. The attitudes which inspired *The Oxford Book of English Verse* to give Donne only as much space as Bulwer Lytton and less than a third as much as Herrick . . . were already under critical fire. After *Prufrock* and the first Pound and Eliot essays, it was becoming increasingly difficult to regard Tennyson or Swinburne as the sole or pre-eminent forces directing English poetry.' In 1958[2] Leavis had already acknowledged that 'Eliot was the man of genius who, after the long post-Swinburnian arrest, altered expression. Such an achievement was possible only to a poet in whom the creative gift was a rare gift of consciousness . . .' As he went on to say in the Epilogue, future English poetry would probably bear the same kind of relation to Eliot 'as later Romantic poetry did to Wordsworth and Coleridge, but for whom Keats and Shelley . . . would possibly not have been poets at all, or if they had been would certainly not have been the poets we know'. This, obviously, was a problem which called for treatment in a separate book, and it was while he was working on *New Bearings* that he conceived *Revaluation*, which was not published until four years later. As he was to write in the Introduction to it: 'The book on modern poetry did in fact take explicit bearings in the past . . . The aim here is to give the full perspective; to complete the account of the present of English poetry with the correlated account of the past.'

How to Teach Reading: A Primer for Ezra Pound was published later in 1932 by Gordon Fraser's Minority Press. In *How to Read*,[3] Pound had made an attempt to 'give a man an orderly arrangement of his perceptions in the matter of taste', and Leavis particularly welcomed his analysis of literature's social function:

> It has to do with maintaining the very cleanliness of the tools, the health of the very matter of thought itself . . . the individual cannot think or communicate his thought, the governor and legislator cannot act effec-

---

[1] His essay on Leavis is reprinted in *Language and Silence*. Faber 1967.
[2] In the essay 'T. S. Eliot as Critic', reprinted in *Anna Karenina and Other Essays*.
[3] Which had been written for the *New York Herald* in 1927 or 1928 and reprinted as a pamphlet in 1931.

tively or frame his laws, without words, and the solidity and validity of
these words is in the care of the damned and despised *literati* . . . when
their very medium, the very essence of their work, the application of
word to thing goes rotten, i.e., becomes slushy and inexact, or excessive
or bloated, the whole machinery of social and of individual thought and
order goes to pot.

He also welcomed Pound's assertion: 'the books that a man needs
to know in order to "get his bearings", in order to have a sound
judgment of any bit of writing that may come before him, are very
few.' Nor is there any difficulty in reconciling the notion of tradition
that Leavis derived from Eliot with Pound's twofold categorization
of important writers: 'a) the *inventors*, "discoverers of a particular
process or of more than one mode and process," and b) the *masters*,
"inventors who, apart from their own inventions, are able to assimi-
late and co-ordinate a large number of preceding inventions."' But
Leavis thought Pound was laying too much stress on the achievement of the individual artist, whereas Eliot, in speaking of 'the mind
of Europe' implied both the consciousness and memory of the
people – the culture in which the literary tradition had developed.

What Leavis found totally unacceptable was the reading list
Pound prescribed for the student. It omitted Shakespeare and Donne
but included Confucius and Homer in full; a Provençal Song Book
with cross references to the Minnesingers and to Bion; Villon;
Voltaire and Gautier. Leavis was not enthusiastic about Pound's
definition of great literature as 'language charged with meaning to the
utmost possible degree', and he quarrelled with Pound's triple
classification of manners in which language can be energized:
Melopoeia, in which words are charged with some musical property,
which directs the trend of their meaning; *Phanopoeia*, which is a
casting of images upon the visual imagination; and *Logopoeia*, which
plays with a word's normal associations. In Leavis's view the three
elements cannot be studied separately, while, in any case, poetic
imagery is not merely visual. To demonstrate this Leavis quoted
from *Macbeth*:

> – All our service
> In every point twice done, and then done double,
> Were poor and single business, to contend
> Against those honours deep and broad, wherewith
> Your majesty loads our house.

After 'contend' has suggested physical force, the image implicit in
'deep and broad' is gradually 'felt rather than seen' to be that of a
'full-flowing and irresistible river'. Deriving the image from the
conventional idea of the King as the 'fount of honour', Shakespeare
has held its realization back from any conflict with the ensuing
image of loading.

In the second part of his essay, under the heading 'Positive
Suggestions', Leavis addresses himself to the problem that is to
preoccupy him throughout his life. How can a university fulfil its
function of providing a sound and liberal education in letters? 'Everything must start from the training of sensibility.' Through practice
in analysis the student can learn 'that literature is made of words,
and that everything worth saying in criticism of verse and prose can
be related to judgments concerning particular arrangements of
words on the page'. I. A. Richards's books provided all the theoretical
apparatus that was required, while *Seven Types of Ambiguity* offered
further education in analysis: 'those who are capable of learning from
it are capable of reading it critically, and those who are not capable
of learning from it were not intended by Nature for an advanced
"education in letters".' (This is to require a great deal from the
school-leaver.) The essays in Eliot's *The Sacred Wood* were exemplary
in their refusal to separate technique from substance.

Discussing 'The Literature of the Present', Leavis formulated a
precept which he was subsequently to ignore: 'a lack of interest in
the present means usually an incapacity for any real interest – the
kind of interest that understands the meaning of "technique" – in
literature at all.' He has had relatively little to say about verse since
Four Quartets and fiction since Lawrence.

He sent a copy of his essay to Pound, who mentioned it in a
letter from Rapallo dated 18 February 1932: 'What is Leavis? He
recently sent me his "Primer"'. Pound thought highly of Denys
Thompson and, in a letter to Ronald Duncan dated 17 January
1939, he wrote: 'Sorry Thompson is Leavising. But can't be helped.'
Pound wrote only one letter to Leavis, who did not offer it for in-
clusion in the collected *Letters*.

This mutual antipathy between two of the most brilliant minds that
have been brought to bear on twentieth-century literature is all the
more regrettable when you consider how much they had in common.
Reviewing Pound's *Letters* in *Scrutiny*,[1] Leavis saluted the intelligence,

[1] XVIII 1 June 1951. The review is reprinted in *Anna Karenina and Other Essays*.

the energy and the public-spiritedness of the Pound who came to England in 1908. 'Never in the literary world, has there been a more courageous single-mindedness.' The sentences he quotes to illustrate it could almost equally well have been penned by Leavis himself: 'It is only when a few men who know get together and *disagree* that any sort of criticism is born.' 'Isn't it worth while having *one* critic who won't say a thing is *good* until he is ready to stake his whole position on the decision?' So could Pound's dictum 'Verse ought to be at least as well written as prose.' If Pound discovered Eliot, Leavis shares some of the credit for establishing his academic reputation, while on Hardy (who greatly influenced him) Pound's final verdict was remarkably close to Leavis's: the 1912–13 poems 'lift him to his apex, sixteen poems from "The Going" to "Castle Boterel", all good, and enough for a lifetime.'[1] Leavis had nothing but admiration for the influence Pound exerted on Yeats, encouraging him 'in his emergence out of the incantations of the Celtic Twilight into speech-rhythms and a use of language spare, taut, and ironical.'

But, for Leavis, much of Pound's criticism was invalidated by his lack of insight into the relationship between language and culture. How could he argue that the reader did not need to be familiar with anything more than 'the few hundred words in the few really good poems that any language has in it'?

---

[1] *Confucius to Cummings.* Edited by Ezra Pound and Marcella Spann. (New Directions. New York 1964.)

4 The Launching of *Scrutiny* and *Revaluation*

The first editors of *Scrutiny* were L. C. Knights, who was doing research into Jacobean comedy, and Donald Culver. After the first two issues, Leavis and Denys Thompson joined the editorial board. The early volumes are remarkable for the breadth of their penetration beyond the main areas of literature and education. In the first issue Goldsworthy Lowes Dickinson wrote on 'The Political Background'; Huxley's *Brave New World* was reviewed by a biologist, Joseph Needham; D. W. Harding's 'A Note on Nostalgia' was mainly literary in its focus, but he also reviewed three new psychology books; J. L. Russell reviewed a philosopher's book about science. In the second issue I. A. Richards contributed an essay on 'The Chinese Renaissance' and Michael Oakeshott wrote on Bentham. W. H. Auden reviewed three educational books, while his *The Orators* was reviewed by Douglas Garman, who had been one of the editors of *The Calendar*. He found the opening prose section interesting but did not feel that the verse justified its obscurity or that the overall organization was adequate.

The first two issues attracted so many subscription orders that from No. 3 onwards, many more copies were printed. William Empson contributed an essay on Marvell's 'The Garden'. Books on music, art, architecture and eugenics were reviewed, as was the first volume of Trotsky's *History of the Russian Revolution*. The editors and Mrs Leavis had not only been preparing copy for the printers, but doing all the work involved in distributing the quarterly – licking stamps and writing addresses. But the fourth issue contains the announcement that the Trinity Street bookshop, Dcighton Bell, was now taking over the distribution. In future, therefore, subscribers would have to pay for the postage – an extra eightpence a year. New contributors included the historian Herbert Butterfield, Edgell Rickword and Geoffrey Grigson, the editor of *New Verse*. A book review by I. A. Richards defended Bentham against Oakeshott's criticism, while W. H. Auden reviewed Winston Churchill's *Thoughts and Adventures*:

> No one reading this book or indeed any by Mr Churchill can credit him with having thought long or deeply about anything, but he is equally ready to write on any subject, the Quantum Theory, Cézanne, or the Old Testament, and except for the title you will not be able to tell which is which.

In the fifth *Scrutiny* (II 1, June 1933) Leavis reviewed new poetry under the title 'This Poetical Renaissance'. He welcomed *New Verse*, recommending readers to support it, although its contents, like those of other English and American poetry magazines, made it impossible to believe in the existence of 'a public in some degree educated about poetry, and capable of appreciating and checking critically the editorial standards; a public embodying a certain collective experience, intelligence and taste.' It was perceptive of Leavis to recognize so early that Empson was 'becoming less and less likely to develop. He seems no nearer than before to finding a more radical incitement to the writing of poetry (or of criticism) than pleasure in a strenuous intellectual game.' The reviewer of Auden's *The Orators* in *The Criterion* had felt 'no doubt that it is the most valuable contribution to English poetry since *The Waste Land*.' Leavis endorsed Garman's verdict that after Auden's earlier volume *Poems*, it was disappointing, marred 'by an unignorable element of something like undergraduate cleverness'. Reviewing Spender's *Poems*, Leavis recognized a genuine talent and an unwitting tendency to reproduce the Meredith of *Modern Love*. In the first of two book reviews dealing with American fiction, Leavis countered over-valuation of Faulkner with the suggestion that his '"technique" is an expression of – or disguise for – an uncertainty about what he is trying to do . . . Faulkner is seldom for long sure of the point of view he is writing from, and will alter his focus and his notation casually, it would seem, and almost without knowing it.' In the other review he used Dos Passos to place Dreiser as a transatlantic equivalent of Arnold Bennett. At the end of the issue is a note of thanks to 'the anonymous donor of £2 "for use in connection with *Scrutiny*"', and, under the title 'The *Scrutiny* Movement in Education', a report on a meeting held in Cambridge. It had started with a statement of aims:

> We have always intended that a positive movement should develop – a movement to propagate and enforce a clearly realized conception of

education and its function. Such a conception, of course, would involve a conception of a desirable society . . .

The political strength of the movement is that it makes an entirely fresh approach to the essential problems of politics – an approach that circumvents old obstacles and impasses, because it goes behind and beneath the inveterate preconceptions and prejudices.

In education . . . the power of the press, of the advertizer and of the literary racket can be challenged as nowhere else. Education, that is, is very unusually practical politics, and without a movement in education it is difficult to take any kind of politics seriously.

Inevitably, the word 'cells' figured in the discussion that ensued. It was agreed that the movement should spread spontaneously with the aid of cues from articles in *Scrutiny*, pamphlets and a leaflet printing the statement of aims. Those who wanted to form groups could obtain copies of the leaflet from the editors.

L. C. Knights's 'Scrutiny of Examinations' in the September issue argued that there was no possibility of reforming the current system of 'wholesale public examination': it should be abolished. 'In examinations involving 5,000 . . . 10,000 . . . 17,000 candidates only facts and standardized opinions can be examined. While the School Certificate, or anything proposing the same function, continues, so long shall we continue "to hale and drag our choicest and hopefullest wits to that asinine feast of sowthistles and brambles which is commonly set before them".' Another revolutionary educational article appeared in the March 1934 issue. In an extended review of George Sampson's *English for the English* Denys Thompson insisted that education could and should 'enable the young to diagnose contemporary civilization and mobilize some impetus to cure it . . . This diagnosis will recognize some left-wing politicians to be as clearly symptoms of a decaying civilization as Sir Oswald Mosley or the Salvation Army, with whom indeed they have much in common – the easy escape, the simple solution, the conviction of self-righteousness.' The educational articles in *Scrutiny* had provoked a lot of letters, one of which had argued: 'the greatest impoverishment that a mechanical life has brought is the lack of personal knowledge from the earliest childhood, of nature and the countryside.' Denys Thompson suggested books that could be helpful, including *Huckleberry Finn, Erewhon*, Cobbett's *Rural Rides* and some of Hardy's novels.

Meanwhile *Culture and Environment*, which was to be reprinted three times during the first ten years of its life, found its way into classrooms all over the country and all over the Commonwealth, influencing not only pupils but teachers with its warning that attention must be paid – and paid critically – to the cultural pressures that determine the way language is used in popular fiction, in journalism and in advertizing. As William Walsh has pointed out, the book 'also helped to prepare an audience able and ready to follow the extra-curricular activities in literary criticism, especially in social analysis and the theory of education. If there has been a audience ready and willing to take to the work, say, of Richard Hoggart or Raymond Williams, this has been because it has been prepared and practised in the necessary, preliminary understanding . . . *Culture and Environment* has sharpened the convictions of several generations of the intelligent young, including a whole cluster of young writers. It has offered them an intellectual stance, a radically critical attitude, and a vocabulary of value capable of being dissolved into their own idiom.'[1]

Leavis's work as an educational revolutionary and critic of contemporary civilization cannot be separated from his work as teacher, writer and editor. All these fields of activity were irrigated by energy that flowed from his conviction that literature, properly studied, could protect language against the depredations of mechanization and commercialism.

Revaluation will survive as a book but, after being drafted verbally in supervisions, it made its first appearance as a series of seven articles in *Scrutiny* between September 1933 and June 1936. What became the first chapter was written for the December 1935 issue as an extended book review: on *The Oxford Book of Seventeenth Century Verse* chosen by H. J. C. Grierson and G. Bullough, and *Rochester: Portrait of a Restoration Poet* by V. de Sola Pinto.

The first chapter to be written was the one on Milton. The book preserves the casually worded opening to the fourth paragraph, which is discussing *Paradise Lost*:

> Here, if this were a lecture, would come illustrative reading-out – say of the famous opening to Book III. As it is, the point seems best enforcible (though it should be obvious at once to anyone capable of being convinced at all) by turning to one of the exceptionally good passages –

He goes on to quote seventeen lines of the Mulciber passage at the end of Book I.[2]

[1] *A Human Idiom: Literature and Humanity*. Chatto 1964.
[2] l. 738 ff.

After so many anti-Miltonic comments, it was high time for Leavis to formulate his criticism in detail. Milton had come under casual critical fire from Pound, Eliot and Middleton Murry, but Eliot's disparaging critique did not appear until 1936, three years later than Leavis's, though, as this points out, the 'irresistible argument' that had effected 'Milton's dislodgment' in the previous decade had been Eliot's poetry. The dismissal of Pound's *Cantos* in *New Bearings* had been unaccompanied by any detailed analysis of characteristic passages; the attack on Milton is far better substantiated, reinforcing its generalizations with practical criticism. In lectures, seminars and supervisions, Leavis must often have employed practical criticism as a tool for demolition, but this is his first negative use of it in a major essay.

One of the lines from *Comus* which comes in for praise is:

Th' earth cumber'd, and the wing'd air dark't with plumes

in which 'the crowding of stressed words, the consonantal clusters and the clogged movement' help to dramatize the situation for the reader, who has a sense of being present – seeing, hearing and feeling. But most of Milton's verse is written in the 'Grand Style', which stiffens the verse, precluding this directness of impact. 'The medium calls pervasively for a kind of attention, compels an attitude towards itself, that is incompatible with sharp, concrete realization; just as it would seem to be, in the mind of the poet, incompatible with an interest in sensuous particularity. He exhibits a feeling *for* words rather than a capacity for feeling *through* words.' Leavis quotes the description of the Garden of Eden in *Paradise Lost* Book IV to illustrate Milton's habit of focusing 'rather upon words than upon perceptions, sensations or things'. T. S. Eliot echoed this point in his 1947 lecture on Milton to the British Academy: 'The emphasis is on the sound, not the vision, upon the word, not the idea.' Discussing Eliot's lecture in *The Sewanee Review*,[1] Leavis apparently forgot that this is how he had himself used the word 'word': 'I find it odd indeed that the author of *Burnt Norton* should have been content to leave us in that way with the word "word "on our hands. What is the "word"? It is certainly not the pure sound – no poet can make us take his verbal arrangements as pure sound, whatever his skill or his genius ... meaning must always enter largely and inseparably into the effect.' But Leavis goes on to make the point very much

[1] I 7, 1949.

more clearly: 'The Miltonic "music" is not the music of the musician; what our "hearing" hears is words; and the sense in which Milton's use of words is characterized by a "musical" bias can be explained only in terms of a generally relaxed state of mind he induces in us. We say that the "emphasis is on the sound" because we are less exactingly conscious in respect of meaning than when we read certain other poets . . . The state induced has analogies with intoxication. Our response brings nothing to any arresting focus, but gives us a feeling of exalted significance, of energetic effortlessness, and of a buoyant ease of command. In return for satisfaction of this order – rhythmic and "musical" – we lower our criteria of force and consistency in meaning.'

Until he wrote the 'Nativity Ode' at the age of twenty-one, Milton had written more in Latin than he had in English. Leavis quotes from Logan Pearsall Smith's *Words and Idioms*: 'This charm of the exceptional and the irregular in diction, accounts for the fact that we can enjoy the use of idiom even in a dead language which we do not know very well; it also explains the subtlety of effect which Milton achieved by transfusing Greek or Latin constructions into his English verse.' As Leavis goes on, 'So complete, and so mechanically habitual, is Milton's departure from the English order, structure and accentuation that he often produces passages that have to be read through several times before one can see how they go, though the Miltonic mind has nothing to offer that could justify obscurity – no obscurity was intended: it is merely that Milton has forgotten the English language.'

Though Eliot was being more polite, he was making a similar point when he suggested in 1936 that 'To extract everything possible from *Paradise Lost*, it would seem necessary to read it in two different ways, first solely for the sound, and second for the sense. The full beauty of his long periods can hardly be enjoyed while we are wrestling with the meaning as well; and for the pleasure of the ear the meaning is hardly necessary, except in so far as certain key-words indicate the emotional tone of the passage.' Leavis had no difficulty in exposing the speciousness of this argument. He had already made the point in 1933 that 'subtlety of movement in English verse depends upon the play of the natural sense movement and intonation against the verse structure, and that "natural" here, involves a reference, more or less direct, to idiomatic speech'. Both Leavis's essays on Milton argue that he 'is not really interested in the achievement of precise thought of any kind; he certainly hasn't the kind of energy of mind needed for sustained analytic and discursive thinking'. A tremendous amount of time has been wasted by students who have pored over Milton's text, encouraged by their teachers to believe that the self-contradiction is only apparent, that theological consistency is to be found, if they dig deeply enough.

Leavis ungrudgingly concedes that the first two books of *Paradise Lost* are 'magnificent in their simple force (party politics in the Grand Style Milton can compass)'. Afterwards, 'though there are intervals of relief', the work becomes 'dull and empty'. Though Leavis emphasizes the remoteness from ordinary speech, he lays less stress in his 1933 essay than Eliot does in his of 1936 on 'the peculiar kind of deterioration' to which Milton 'subjected the language':

> Milton's poetry could *only* be an influence for the worse, upon any poet whatever . . . Milton's bad influence may be traced much farther than the eighteenth century, and much farther than upon bad poets . . . it was an influence against which we still have to struggle.

Retracting these assertions in 1947, Eliot made a spurious and disingenuous claim. He summed up his earlier contentions as:

1. good poets in the 18th and 19th centuries would have written better but for Milton's influence;
2. The contemporary situation was such that Milton was a master who should be avoided;
3. the influence of Milton, or of any particular poet can be *always* bad.

He was no longer prepared to make the first or third assertion, he said, because without the second they were meaningless. It is obvious that the first is not in the least dependent on the second, and I think Leavis was right to argue that Eliot's recantation and his 'speciously judicial refusal to judge' brought him close to 'a surrender of the function of criticism'. Could Keats have written his mature Odes if he hadn't abandoned his first *Hyperion* with the comment 'Milton's verse cannot be written but in an artful, or rather, artist's humour'? As Leavis goes on to argue, Milton's influence is also to be found in Tennyson, who wanted to bring English as near to the Italian as possible, and in Matthew Arnold, for whom poetry differed from prose 'in not imposing any strict intellectual criterion'. (How else could such an intelligent man 'have been capable, when writing verse, of such weak confusion, such intellectual debility'?)

The chapters on Pope, Wordsworth, Shelley and Keats were

Leavis's four contributions to the first nine of a series called 'Revaluations', which may have been inspired by the series of 'Scrutinies' in *The Calendar*, though these were all reassessments of contemporary writers. Although Leavis's *Revaluation* would obviously be different if he had written it as a book, he had conceived it as a book, four years previously, and the essay on 'English Poetry in the 18th Century' (*Scrutiny* V 1, June 1936) would probably never have been written if it had not been destined to become Chapter Four, 'The Augustan Tradition'.

The Pope essay[1] is complementary to the one on Milton in showing how formal exaltation of manner can be combined with flexibility both of attitude and of versification. As Leavis suggests, there was a rare maturity in Pope's sensibility that allowed him to tread wittily along the verge of the ludicrous, mixing his tones enough to keep the reader alert but never enough to upset balance, destroy continuity or violate decorum. 'Elegy to the Memory of an Unfortunate Lady' allows full play to Pope's critical intelligence. If the critic who is a poet tends to be most attracted to the poetry that gives him most help in writing his own, the critic who is not may tend to be most fascinated by the poetry that has the merits of good criticism. Leavis always responds most readily to the implicit evaluation of an emotion or experience by 'placing' it in relation to a considered scale of values. But the essay on Pope emphasizes the point that it was not merely as a satirist that he succeeded. The diversity of his achievement was most impressive.

It is, as Leavis suggests, 'plain enough that Pope's reconciliation of Metaphysical wit with the Polite has antecedents' – a sentence which will have more force when the essay becomes the third chapter in a book which begins with a chapter on Donne and the seventeenth-century 'Line of Wit'. But the technique is characteristic of Leavis: to define representative qualities by looking backwards as well as forwards and to concentrate on the great writers with whom this can be done.

The stress on Pope's variety, flexibility and versatility is not allowed to obscure the fact that he was 'pre-eminently a satirist', and Leavis defends him against the customary charge of venomous envy:

> There is, indeed, evidence in the satires of strong personal feelings, but even – or, rather, especially – where these appear strongest, what (if we are literate) we should find most striking is an intensity of art . . . When

[1] *Scrutiny* II 4, December 1933.

Pope contemplates the bases and essential conditions of Augustan culture his imagination fires to a creative glow that produces what is poetry even by Romantic standards. His contemplation is religious in its seriousness. . . . His technique, concerned as it is with arranging words and 'regulating' movements, is the instrument of a fine organization, and it brings to bear pressures and potencies that can turn intense personal feelings into something else.

He moves with urbane speed from vitriolic satire to sober worship of contemporary civilization, perceived as parallel with (and expressive of) 'an ultimate and inclusive order'. Leavis quotes the couplet

> Ask you what Provocation I have had?
> The strong Antipathy of Good to Bad[1]

which does not adequately suggest the moral basis of Pope's satire but does remind us that 'his strength as a satirist was that he lived in an age when such an account could be offered.'

Eliot's 'Homage to John Dryden' (1921) had been paid partly at the expense of Pope. Leavis's revaluation applies the techniques of practical criticism to demonstrate that Pope is the better poet. The end of the *Dunciad* is superior to any comparable passage of *Mac-Flecknoe* in intensity and taut sensitivity. The reader can make his own comparison between the ten lines of Dryden Eliot quotes on page 311 of *Selected Essays* and the fourteen lines from the *Dunciad* Leavis quotes on page 87 of *Revaluation*. Pope is no less creative and much more amusing, but Leavis is right to suggest that *The Rape of the Lock* has had more attention than it deserves. So has *The Essay on Man*: 'he cannot, as Dryden can, argue interestingly in verse.' Leavis's revaluation rests mainly on the *Epistles* and the fourth book of the *Dunciad*, which, as he phrases it in his later essay on the *Dunciad*,[2] 'enlists Milton into an Augustan sublime'. The essay also warns students not to let scholarly annotation get in the way of the poetry. 'Pope has created something the essential interest of which lies within itself, in what it is.'

With Wordsworth[3] it was necessary to show that his genius was inhospitable to the philosophical ambition that Coleridge encouraged. Book II of *The Prelude*, for instance, is deceptive in appearing to present a paraphrasable argument. Wordsworth's 'triumph is to com-

---

[1] Epilogue to the Satires, Dialogue II.
[2] *Scrutiny* XLL 1, Winter 1943, reprinted in *The Common Pursuit*.
[3] *Scrutiny* III 3, December 1934.

mand the kind of attention he requires and to permit no other . . .
The expository effect sorts well with – blends into – the characteristic meditative gravity of the emotional presentment ("emotion recol-
lected in tranquillity"), and in the key passages, where significance
seems specially to reside, the convincing success of the poetry covers
the argument.' The influence that Wordsworth exerted on the lives
of John Stuart Mill and Leslie Stephen derived not from his philosophy but from his wisdom, which was 'sufficiently presented in the
body of his living work', as he tacitly recognized by leaving the
great 'philosophic poem' unfinished. His 'preoccupation was with a
distinctively human naturalness, with sanity and spiritual health',
though the mode of that preoccupation was characteristic of 'a mind
intent always upon ultimate sanctions, and upon the living connec-
tions between man and the extra-human universe; it was, that is,
in the same sense as Lawrence's was, religious', the overriding concern being 'with the deep levels, the springs of life, the illimitable
mystery that wells up into consciousness'. Leavis cites Lawrence's
belief that a 'wise passiveness' was in fact a concentrated activity
and a very useful one: 'that which is perfectly ourselves can take
place in us'. Leavis also points backwards, reminding us that
Wordsworth's 'essential sanity and normality' had deep roots in the
eighteenth century. David Nichol Smith's Preface to his *Oxford Book
of 18th Century Verse* had quoted a passage of Mark Akenside (1721–
70), validly suggesting that it could be mistaken for Wordsworth.

Leavis could have made more use of this point in defending him
against Shelley's 'Peter Bell the Third', which mocks him as 'a kind
of moral eunuch . . . a solemn and unsexual man.' Certainly the
verse displays 'an impersonality unknown to Shelley', but Leavis
does not solve the problem posed by the erotic self-denial of Wordsworth's poetry with the point that his spontaneity supervenes on complex development. 'He stands for a distinctly human naturalness; one,
that is, consummating a discipline, moral and other.' But it is useful –
and it was even more useful in the mid-thirties – to draw the emphasis
away from the 'visionary' element in Wordsworth's work. He sometimes describes semi-mystical experiences, but the critic can best
establish their significance 'not by dwelling upon or in them, in the
hope of exploring something that lies hidden in or behind their
vagueness, but by holding firmly on to that sober verse in which they
are presented'. A comparison of 'Simplon Pass' with 'Mont Blanc' is
revealing. The opening shows that Shelley was willing to borrow

from Wordsworth; the development shows him to be incapable of preserving a Wordsworthian equilibrium in treating visionary experience.

In Leavis's view Wordsworth's finest poetry is to be found in Book I of *The Excursion*, which incorporates *Margaret; or The Ruin'd Cottage* (1795–7), in *Michael* (1800) and in the *Immortality Ode* (1803–6). *Michael* is characteristic of this early period: painful experiences are put into the past and held 'at such a distance that serenity, for all the pathos, never falters; and an idealizing process, making subtle use of the mountain background, gives to "human suffering" a reconciling grandeur.' But Wordsworth depended so heavily on experiences that belonged to his childhood and youth that his later poetry was increasingly debilitated by his increasing distance from them. The public voice becomes 'a substitute for the inner voice ... For the sentiments and attitudes of the patriotic and Anglican Wordsworth do not come as the intimately and particularly realized experience of an unusually and finely conscious individual; they are external, general and conventional; their quality is that of the medium they are proffered in, which is insensitively Miltonic, a medium not felt into from within as something at the nerve-tips, but handled from outside.' In 'the pursuit of formal orthodoxy' the older Wordsworth was liable to falsify the experiences recorded in *The Prelude*. Although Leavis acknowledges this, he prefers the 1850 version of *The Prelude* to the early version (1805–6). Comparing the two treatments of the passage that starts 'Bless'd the infant Babe', he comments: 'No one is likely to dispute that the later version is decidedly the more satisfactory,' and he finds it less explicit. I find it more explicit and I think the one major weakness in Leavis's excellent essay derives from his failure to recognize that the earlier version of *The Prelude* is generally superior to the 1850 revision, which seems to me more ponderous, less fresh, less vivid and less direct.

Shelley's poetic pulse is faster, more feverish than Milton's, but they both depend on sweeping the reader into a submissive unconcern with meaning. Just as Eliot has exposed the inconsistencies in Milton's imagery by asking unanswerable questions, Leavis's essay on Shelley[1] challenges the 'Ode to the West Wind': 'In what respects are the "loose clouds" like "decaying leaves"? ... What again, are those "tangled boughs of Heaven and Ocean"? ... Then again, in what ways does the approach of a storm ("loose clouds like earth's

[1] *Scrutiny* IV 2, September 1935.

decaying leaves," "like ghosts from an enchanter fleeing") suggest streaming Hair?' In the 'general tendency of the images to forget the status of the metaphor or simile that introduced them and to assume an autonomy and a right to propagate, so that we lose in confused generations and perspectives the perception or thought that was the ostensible *raison d'être* of imagery, we have a recognized essential trait of Shelley's: his weak grasp upon the actual.' Wordsworth 'seems always to be presenting an object (wherever this may belong) and the emotion seems to derive from what is presented'; for Shelley, being inspired was 'too apt to mean surrendering to a kind of hypnotic rote of favourite images, associations and words'. Like much of his work, 'To a Skylark' is 'a mere tumbled out spate ("spontaneous overflow") of poeticalities, the place of each one of which Shelley could have filled with another without the least difficulty and without making any essential difference. They are held together by the pervasive "lyrical emotion", and that this should be capable of holding them together is comment enough on the nature of its strength.'

The book review that became Chapter 1, 'The Line of Wit' brilliantly illuminates the territory that Eliot would have surveyed in detail if he had not abandoned his project for a book on The School of Donne. Leavis, of course, stresses the affinities with Shakespeare in the 'mastery of tone', the inexhaustible 'subtleties of Donne's use of the speaking voice and the spoken language', the dramatization of situations and the way Donne plays his sense-movement across the verse lines. But 'Donne is writing something original and quite different from blank verse. For all their apparent casualness, the rimes, it should be plain, are strictly used; the couplet-structure, though not in Pope's way, is functional.'

The essay on Keats[1] became the final chapter of the book. It was necessary in 1936 to contradict John Middleton Murry (who thought the poems could best be used 'to elucidate the deep and natural movement of the poet's soul') and Arthur Symons (who saw Keats as a precursor of the nineties, a man 'to whom art is more than life'). Comparison with Shelley's 'To a Skylark' shows how finely Keats constructed his 'Ode to a Nightingale'. Symons was quite wrong to say 'He saw words as things, and he saw them one at a time.' Applying practical criticism to the Ode, Leavis demonstrates its subtle interplay of emotions: 'it moves outwards and upwards towards life

[1] *Scrutiny* IV 4, March 1936.

as strongly as it moves downwards towards extinction.' But it is not a great poem that can stand up to frequent re-reading. 'It is as if Keats were making major poetry out of minor – as if, that is, the genius of a major poet were working in the material of minor poetry.' What is disappointing about Leavis's essay is that instead of sub-stantiating this value-judgment, he turns away from the poetry to spend a good deal of his limited space on the Victorian aesthetes who 'made creedal or liturgical use' of the equation between truth and beauty that comes at the end of 'Ode on a Grecian Urn'. In compensation, his analyses of the 'Ode on Melancholy' and 'To Autumn' show how un-Swinburnian and un-Tennysonian they are, with their sensuous firmness and their tactile images. Predictably, Leavis is also good on the transition from the first *Hyperion* to *The Fall of Hyperion*. If the earlier version is 'Miltonic as transformed by a taste for "Spenserian vowels that elope with ease" (the ease of this verse is languorous and luxurious)', the later verse 'moves line by line, the characteristic single line having, as it were, an evenly dis-tributed weight – a settled quite unspringy balance.' There is no afflatus and no emotional self-indulgence. 'As a result, his response, his attitude, seems to us to inhere in the facts, and to have itself the authenticity of fact.'

The last of the seven essays, 'English Poetry in the 18th Century', was published in *Scrutiny* V 1 (June 1936). Retitled 'The Augustan Tradition and the 18th Century', it occupies the central position in *Revaluation*, bridging between the chapters on Pope and Wordsworth. Something had gone wrong with the development of English poetry. Edgell Rickword dated the bad period as lasting from 1720 to 1780, and, as Leavis says, a tradition that does not make good use of minor talent 'may be suspected of having also confined major talent to minor performance'. Miltonic magniloquence was being channelled into genteel elegiacs.

Leavis's balanced, useful criticism of Gray shows that it is not only in dealing with major writers that he is at his best. He recog-nizes the strength in Gray's conventionality: the success of his 'Elegy' 'is a triumph not so much of creative talent as of taste', but the 'churchyard meditations have, as it were, social substance'. He is less generous towards *The Seasons*. 'Thomson's declamatory Mil-tonics ... depart consciously from Augustan technique and idiom, but, departing consciously, they never forget: their bardic nobility pays involuntary homage to the neatness and prose propriety they

offer a holiday from.' Like most of Gray's work, like Dyer's, Akenside's and Shenstone's, they belong to a monotonous tributary of
mainstream verse. The recurrent words are 'sequestered', 'mouldered'
(or 'mouldering'), 'contemplation', 'pensive', and 'votary'. Without
placing any higher valuation on Collins, Leavis concedes that his
'Ode to Evening' belongs distinctively to the eighteenth century 'in
achieving a remarkable freedom from the Augustan – from the
suggestions, in its idiom and movement, of social deportment and
polite civilization.'

But even in the high Augustan period, how much verse was there
that could be ranked beside Pope's? Swift was not a major poet
and he made the Augustan positives look like negatives. Prior was
not only less original but out of touch with the 'line of wit'.

> It is not merely that sensibility has changed; senses and faculties have
> been lost, a perceptive and responsive organization has ceased to func-
> tion, a capacity for fineness has disappeared . . . As a result of the Social
> and economic changes speeded up by the Civil War, a metropolitan
> fashionable Society, compact and politically in the ascendant, found
> itself in charge of standards . . . If we say that the age was one in which
> the code of Good Form was in intimate touch with the most serious
> cultural code we indicate limitations and strength at the same time . . .
> the ease, elegance and regularity favoured belong, we feel, to the realm
> of manners; the diction, gesture and deportment of the verse observe a
> polite social code. . . . Restoration polite culture . . . had no serious
> relations with the moral bases of society.

Compared with Pope's Augustanism, the essence of Johnson's was
'more a feeling for a literary order, and less a feeling for any social
order that pressed immediately upon him . . . His sense of form was
a sense of a traditional morality of his craft, enjoining an artistic and
intellectual discipline.' Unlike Pope's, his writing 'does not feel
within close range a polite, conversing society'. Leavis compares
Johnson's 'On the Death of Mr Robert Levett' with Cowper's 'The
Castaway', the affinities lying in 'declamatory decorum' and 'precise and patterned rationality of statement'.

Before the essay ends, Leavis has worked in references to Blake,
Crabbe and Byron, who 'had strong conscious sympathies with the
Augustan tradition', though his satirical verse was 'not in any
Augustan mode'. None of the essays reappears in the book without
having a few pages of notes added; this chapter has nine notes,
which occupy 24 pages. Spenser, Landor and Coleridge are intro-

duced, almost as if Leavis were reaching out towards a more comprehensive account of English poetry than his method allows him.

Revaluation is an important book, which succeeds in consolidating the achievement of *New Bearings*, while providing better evidence of Leavis's overall superiority to Eliot as a critic. In his 1958 critique of Eliot's criticism[1] he makes some severely limiting judgments about Eliot's critical practice. 'There is, of course, value-judgment (though not an appraisal of, say, Donne or Marvell or Dryden) entailed in the very effectively directed critical observations by which he established a general taste for the Metaphysicals and a general understanding of its relevance to the appreciation of his own creative achievement ... He made some stimulating observations about dramatic verse and the conventions of poetic drama, but no radically intelligent – no truly critical – appraisal of any of the Elizabethans or Jacobeans; he has done, in fact, nothing to disturb at all seriously, where Elizabethan–Jacobean drama is in question, the institutional valuation coming down from Lamb and Swinburne; rather, he has confirmed its inflationary habit.' Leavis's own appraisals are truly critical. As he says in the Introduction to *Revaluation*, 'In dealing with individual poets the rule of the critic is, or should (I think) be, to work as much as possible in terms of particular analysis – analysis of poems or passages, and to say nothing that cannot be related immediately to judgments about producible texts. Observing this rule and practising this self-denial the critic limits, of course, his freedom; but there are kinds of freedom he should not aspire to, and the discipline, while not preventing his saying anything that he should in the end find himself needing to say, enables him to say it with a force of relevance and an edged economy not otherwise attainable.' It is because he succeeded in imposing this discipline on himself that *Revaluation* is such an important book, cogently substantiating its delineation of the central tradition in English poetry as leading from Shakespeare to the Metaphysical poets and by-passing Milton on its way to Pope, the Augustans, Wordsworth, Shelley and Keats.

This discipline of specific analysis and self-denial, saying nothing that cannot be related immediately to judgments about producible texts, is a discipline that Eliot – banker, poet, essayist, publisher, editor and playwright – never needed to cultivate. Leavis would have been unable to cultivate it so successfully if he had not been teaching.

[1] 'T. S. Eliot as a Critic'.

He dedicated *Revaluation* to Downing College and ended his Introduction with the sentence 'The debt that I wish to acknowledge is to
those with whom I have, during the past dozen years, discussed
literature as a "teacher": if I have learnt anything about the methods
of profitable discussion I have learnt it in collaboration with them.'
This is not just a polite formula, and it is not invalidated by the
memories of students who recall that he did nearly all the talking
during their supervisions. What Leavis said of Wittgenstein was also
true of himself: 'He had found very few clever and willing persons
who proved capable of engaging in real spoken exchange with him.
Nevertheless he needed, as everyone does – geniuses are not exempt –
a measure of collaborative human presence – presence of which he
could be conscious as proof of a human interest other than his
immediate personal own in the aims and methods he was verifying
and refining as he battled with himself to make them acceptably
articulate. The "collaborative", of course, is implied in the "own" –
as it is in the "make articulate" and the "acceptably". His "lectures"
were his discussions.' I don't know whether Wittgenstein was a
good teacher; that Leavis was is proved by the achievements of his
students. Even creative writers were helped, as Thom Gunn acknowledged when he said that Leavis's criticism of Shelley helped one
'to hold in leash, or to a certain extent transform, one's own self-pity'.

Scrutiny's financial margins were extremely narrow. To raise money
for it, the contributors to *Determinations* all agreed that the rights
could be sold to Chatto and Windus for a lump sum, while the
Leavises, besides filling their lives with unpaid editorial and secre-
tarial work, were effectively subsidizing the quarterly with their own
money. Mrs Leavis, who did a large share of the work, was never
officially on the editorial board. D. W. Harding, who replaced
Donald Culver on it after the June 1933 issue (II 1) remaining one
of the four editors until the spring of 1947 (XIV 3) recently said 'it
was very much a hand-to-mouth affair. There was a time when
Leavis even wrote round, I remember, to the rest of us on the editorial board and said that he'd be grateful if we could contribute a
little towards the postal expenses. The money that was coming in
wasn't really covering his expenses and of course he was hard up too.
I remember I managed to scrape up £2 – this was out of a salary of
£350 in my first university post. But this was the way we were run-

ning. We really were in very great difficulties all the time. And then the other difficulty that Leavis met constantly was the difficulty of getting contributions of the quality he wanted. And each issue was more or less a crisis. He was never sure until the last moment whether there would be enough to fill the issue and often of course he had to write for an issue very much more than he'd intended and write it much faster than he'd intended.'

Unlike his wife, Leavis has never found it easy to write. Once, when W. H. Mellers was staying in their house while studying for his Mus.B. after taking a degree in English, Leavis complained with wry envy about the speed at which his wife and Mellers could both write.

Reviewing Auden's *The Dance of Death* and the new edition of his *Poems* in June 1934, Leavis credited him with possessing 'just what Mr Empson appears to lack: a profound inner disturbance; a turbid pressure of emotions from below; a tension of impulsive life too urgent and shifting to permit him the sense of intellectual mastery'. But if Empson's verse was overworked, Auden's 'blend of surface poise and fundamental self-mistrust would seem to indicate the need for a peculiarly resolute critical effort on the part of the poet', an effort Auden was not making. The obscurities in *Paid on Both Sides* were sustained by intensity of feeling 'but in the accompanying poems the freedoms of transition and private association appear altogether too casual, and there is no evidence of any sustained intensity of preoccupation with technique'. That Leavis was liable to place too much emphasis on the virtues of intellectual control is evidenced by his over-valuation of Ronald Bottrall as a poet, but while there is too much Bottrall among the little verse that *Scrutiny* published in its first eleven volumes – there was none after the war – it did make a contribution towards rescuing Isaac Rosenberg from neglect by printing five of his unpublished poems (in March 1935) together with a thoughtful essay by D. W. Harding, arguing that far from 'clothing a thought in language', Rosenberg 'brought language to bear on the incipient thought at an earlier stage of its development. Instead of the emerging idea being racked slightly so as to fit a more familiar approximation of itself, and words found for that, Rosenberg let it manipulate words almost from the beginning, often without insisting on the controls of logic and intelligibility.' In a *Poetry Bookshop Chapbook* T. S. Eliot mentioned Rosenberg as a poet who would have received more attention if criticism

had been performing its function. But he did nothing else to help.
D. W. Harding and Gordon Bottomley edited a complete edition of
Rosenberg's works, which was published in 1937 by Chatto. Reviewing it in *Scrutiny*, Leavis called Rosenberg a genius whose interest in
life was 'radical and religious in the same sense as D. H. Lawrence's'.

It was in March 1935 that Leavis turned decisively against I. A.
Richards, condemning his new book *Coleridge on Imagination*. Two
years previously in *Scrutiny*, D. W. Harding had argued that the view
we take of Richards's work must depend on our attitude to his belief
that the value of any activity depends on the degree to which it
allows of a balancing or ordering among one's impulses. From
Principles of Literary Criticism onwards, Richards had made Benthamite
assumptions about the satisfaction that art could provide – the more
impulses it gratified the better – and it was inevitable that Leavis
should feel obliged to attack a book that tried to use Bentham's
Theory of Fictions and Coleridge's philosophical writing as two
stepping stones towards a new science. Richards's 1926 book *Poetry
and Science* had tried, rather uncomfortably, to justify a place for
poetry in a world that was daily becoming more scientific in its
orientation. Poetry, he claimed, could save us from the chaos caused
by the development of psychology. Leavis's attack on the Coleridge
book is comparable to his much later, much more famous attack on
C. P. Snow's idea of a separate, scientific culture. He accused
Richards of being unable to make up his mind whether science and
poetry were two different kinds of thing or fundamentally the same
kind of thing – both 'myths' or 'mythologies'. The book was riddled
with imprecision: Richards was neither using words carefully enough
in formulating his generalizations nor substantiating his statements
about myths with critical analysis. In wanting to make Coleridge's
distinction between Imagination and Fancy into a test that could be
applied as in a laboratory experiment, Richards was aiming at a
precision that excluded the kind of non-scientific analysis which it
was the critic's main function to offer. But the most interesting point
of all in this 1935 disagreement between them involves the phrase
'linguistic analysis'. Coleridge, according to Richards, took us

> across the threshold of a general theoretical study of language capable of
> opening to us new powers over our minds comparable to those which
> systematic critical inquiries are giving us over our environment . . .
> It requires the shift from a preoccupation with the What and Why to
> the How of language . . . And it has this consequence, that critics in the

future must have a theoretical equipment of a kind which has not been felt to be necessary in the past . . . But the critical equipment will not be primarily philosophical. It will be rather a command of the methods of general linguistic analysis.

This is oddly prophetic, but Leavis was right to object that *Coleridge on Imagination* neither clarified the nature of the new science nor laid the foundations of a mathematical approach to it.

Meanwhile Sir Arthur Quiller-Couch was becoming increasingly convinced that Tillyard and Henn, who went on for years alternating between the Chairmanship and Secretaryship of the Faculty Board, were discriminating unfairly against Leavis. 'Q' began to intervene on his behalf, but his first attempts were abortive. Tillyard, who was always on the board that made the appointments, was a clever strategist. It was only with coaching from Leavis that 'Q' was finally able to out-manoeuvre him. The vacancy Leavis was to fill had been created by Forbes's death; though Forbes's appointment had been full-time, Leavis's was only part-time. But he achieved a greater degree of financial security when Downing awarded him a fellowship. He was now forty-one.

5   Philosophy and Pre-war Politics

Leavis has often been attacked for refusing to define the criteria that underlie his judgments. One of the earliest and friendliest of these attacks came in a letter from the American literary theorist René Wellek, who offered his own extrapolation of the 'assumptions' behind *Revaluation* by taking some of Leavis's phrases out of their context:

> Allow me to sketch your ideal of poetry, your 'norm' with which you measure every poet: your poetry must be in serious relation to actuality, it must have a firm grasp of the actual, of the object, it must be in relation to life, it must not be cut off from direct vulgar living, it should be normally human, testify to spiritual health and sanity, it should not be personal in the sense of indulging in personal dreams and fantasies, there should be no emotion for its own sake in it, no afflatus, no mere generous emotionality, no luxury in pain or joy, but also no sensuous poverty, but a sharp, concrete realization, a sensuous particularity. The language of your poetry must not be cut off from speech, should not flatter the singing voice, should not be merely mellifluous, should not give e.g. a mere general sense of motion, etc.

In March 1937 the 8-page letter was published in *Scrutiny*, and in June Leavis made some important formulations in his 12-page reply:

> Words in poetry invite us, not to 'think about' and judge but to 'feel into' or 'become' – to realize a complex experience that is given in the words. They demand, not merely a fuller-bodied response, but a completer responsiveness – a kind of responsiveness that is incompatible with the judicial, one-eye-on-the-standard approach suggested by Dr Wellek's phrase: 'your "norm" with which you measure every poet.' The critic – the reader of poetry – is indeed concerned with evaluation, but to figure him as measuring with a norm which he brings up to the object and applies from the outside is to misrepresent the process.

If his norm is brought from inside, it must be inseparable from his personality, which is inseparable from the totality of his experience, in so far as he has interiorized it. And, as Leavis says, 'His first concern is to enter into possession of the given poem (let us say) in its concrete fulness, and his constant concern is never to lose his completeness of possession, but rather to increase it. In making value-judgments (and judgments as to significance), implicitly or explicitly, he does so out of that completeness of possession and with that fulness of response. He doesn't ask, "How does this accord with these specifications of goodness in poetry?"; he aims to make fully conscious and articulate the immediate sense of value that "places" the poem.' As he goes on, 'the process of "making fully conscious and articulate" is a process of reacting and organizing, and the "immediate sense of value" should, as the critic matures with experience, represent a growing stability of organization'. This is a way in which reading contributes to the development of the personality towards maturity. Explicit statements about values are usually too clumsy to be useful, but, as a counter to the generalizations Wellek was proffering, Leavis did make one statement about the relation between poetry and actuality: 'traditions, or prevailing conventions or habits, that tend to cut poetry in general off from direct vulgar living and the actual, or that make it difficult for the poet to bring into poetry his most serious interests as an adult living in his own time, have a de-vitalizing effect.' And, as Leavis insists, 'I do not, again, argue in general terms that there should be "no emotion for its own sake, no afflatus, no mere generous emotionality, no luxury in pain and joy" but by choice, arrangement and analysis of concrete examples I give those phrases (in so far, that is, as I have achieved my purpose) a precision of meaning they couldn't have got in any other way.'

No critic can put paid to the possibility that confusion will arise when aesthetic ideas are plucked out of their critical context or philosophical ideas out of their literary context, but Leavis has probably done more than any other writer to clarify the dangers. His essay on 'Tragedy and the Medium – A Note on Mr Santayana's Tragic Philosophy'[1], is extremely useful as a formulation about the interplay of pressures between words and ideas. Even a critic as good as D. W. Harding is liable to slip into the fallacious assumption that the functioning of all but the greatest writers can be described in terms of clothing a thought in language – as if the idea were totally formed before the words were found for it. A writer does not begin by deciding what his 'message' is going to be and proceed to find a way of expressing it. Shakespeare is the supreme example of the poet whose manipulation of words is inseparable from his manipulation

[1] *Scrutiny* XII 4, Autumn 1944.

of 'a complex dramatic theme vividly and profoundly realized – not thought of, but possessed imaginatively in its concreteness, so that, as it grows in specificity, it in turn possesses the poet's mind and commands expression'. The organization of material has its 'local life' in the verse.

To discuss literature in terms of 'ideas' or 'philosophical content' is to ignore the question of what it is that makes a text come to life for the reader. The writer's creativity can be sterilized by uncreative reading. As Leavis says,[1]

> We can have the poem only by an inner kind of possession; it is 'there' for analysis only in so far as we are responding appropriately to the words on the page. In pointing to them (and there is nothing else to point to) what we are doing is to bring into sharp focus, in turn, this, that and the other detail, juncture or relation in our total response; or (since 'sharp focus' may be a misleading account of the kind of attention sometimes required), what we are doing is to dwell with a deliberate, considering responsiveness on this, that or the other mode or focal point in the complete organization that the poem is, in so far as we have it. Analysis is not a dissection of something that is already and passively there. What we call analysis is, of course, a constructive or creative process. It is a more deliberate following-through of that process of creation in response to the poet's words which reading is.

The disadvantage of fighting without a philosophical banner is that you tend to fight on your own. Leavis was a formidable freelance until arrows started to shower in on him from all sides after his attack on C. P. Snow. It was only then that he felt unable to go on without a philosophical ally and began to fight under Michael Polanyi's banner. Not much of his best criticism belongs to this late period, but what is remarkable is that he fought alone for so long.

Looking back today on the whole corpus of Leavis's literary and cultural criticism, it seems obvious that his achievement is far greater than it could have been if he had chosen to adumbrate his values philosophically. An agnostic with temperamental leanings towards the Puritan virtues of seriousness and self-control, he has produced a body of work which proceeded organically and coherently from attitudes which did not remain static. Refusing to specialize in one medium or one period, he went on reading widely in the poetry

---

[1] 'Literary Studies' in *Scrutiny* IX 4, March 1941, reprinted in *Education and the University*.

and prose of four centuries, developing as he read, remaining open to the possibility of revising his opinions.

The most distinguished attempt at categorizing him and *Scrutiny* was made in 1941, when T. S. Eliot, addressing the Malvern Conference, described the editorial policy as 'humanist'. Referring to Leavis's 1934 article 'Why Universities?' Eliot quoted the proposition that 'the problem of producing the "educated man" – the man of humane culture who is equipped to be intelligent and responsible about the problems of contemporary civilization – becomes that of realizing the Idea of a University in practical dispositions appropriate to the modern world'. He agreed that it was urgently necessary 'to explore the means of bringing the various kinds of specialist knowledge and training into effective relation with informed general intelligence, humane culture, social conscience and political will'. His objection is: 'But to such questions as "Why should we want humane culture? Why is one conception of humane culture better than another? What is the sanction for your conception of social conscience or of political will as against that, for instance, now dominant in Germany?" I do not think that the humanist can give a satisfactory answer. Not every system of theology can lead us to an answer either.' If many of us would now feel that the collected works of Leavis would provide a better answer than any system of theology, this is not in spite of his refusal to rise to such bait as Wellek threw out but because of that refusal.

It was equally necessary to hold back from political commitment. In 1932 Leavis had already made the point 'that one does not necessarily take one's social and political responsibilities the less seriously because one is not quick to see salvation in a formula or in any simple creed'. In his article 'Under Which King, Bezonian?' he quoted Edmund Wilson's *New Statesman* article of 15 October: 'it is surprising how promptly the writers are lining up in one or other of the camps, and how readily their antagonisms are developing.' Wilson was full of approval; Leavis was suspicious 'not only that the appeal of the chic has something to do with it, but that the differences are not of a kind that has much to do with thinking'. He noticed that T. S. Eliot's commitment to Royalism and Anglo-Catholicism was not preventing him from rallying fashionable Marxists to publication in *The Criterion*.

The positions that intellectuals were adopting are represented in *The Mind in Chains*, which was published in 1937, edited by Cecil

Day Lewis, who maintained 'that the mind is really in chains today, that these chains have been forged by a dying social system, that they can and must be broken – and in the Soviet Union have been broken'. Edward Upward declared: 'In Russia already writers are better off than anywhere else in the world,' while Edgell Rickword, who had been anything but naïve in the twenties, wrote: 'In the new civilization of the Soviet Union "government by the people for the people", that ghost which haunts the capitalist democracies with the reminder of their youthful promises, becomes a living reality based on the right of all to work and to leisure.' To Leavis the Marxist challenge seemed to be 'as heroic as Ancient Pistol's and to point to as real alternatives'. *Scrutiny* would aim not to offer solutions but to insist that problems should be faced squarely, while Trotsky, like Marxists of today, was ducking the problem of continuity between pre-revolutionary and post-revolutionary culture. He was using the word culture with a disingenuous vagueness when he said: 'The proletariat acquires power for the purpose of doing away with class culture and to make way for human culture.' The view Leavis took was more historical: 'The process of civilization that produced, among other things, the Marxian dogma, and makes it plausible, has made the cultural difference between the "classes" inessential. The essential differences are indeed now definable in economic terms, and to aim at solving the problems of civilization in terms of the "class war" is to aim, whether wittingly or not, at completing the work of capitalism and its products, the cheap car, the wireless and the cinema.'

The main target for *Scrutiny*'s assaults in the thirties was not the Fascists but the Philistines. Leavis believed that only a small minority could benefit from advanced education in literature; so, even when war became more imminent, *Scrutiny* could hardly have been expected to adopt a friendly attitude towards the Left Book Club. Harold Laski was claiming: 'We are fighting here in this club to maintain the traditions of civilization,' while the group organizer, Dr Lewis, was using the phrase 'Left Wing University'. Sponsored by Laski, Victor Gollancz and John Strachey, the club was offering not only cheap books but summer conferences, and it had recruited a membership of over forty thousand.

'When one has passed a much lower figure,' objected H. A. Mason in his *Scrutiny* article 'Education by Book Club',[1] 'one has
[1] VI 3, December 1937.

exhausted the number of those who at the moment are prepared to study seriously what the L.B.C. can offer. If the surplus is to be retained and given "value for money", something less austere must be provided. Consequently we find assurances (reminiscent of the Book Society's worst) that such and such a book is "as easy to read and understand as any novel from the circulating library", or "is as exciting and thrilling in parts as a wild west novel".' Mason was employing the 'anthropological' approach advocated and adopted by *Fiction and the Reading Public*, and when a letter from Boris Ford objected that he was ignoring the international crisis, Mason's reply was reinforced by an editorial statement in the issue of May 1938: 'We believe that, though crises may very well make it impossible to go on contending on behalf of critical standards and critical intelligence, there is no more urgent duty than to go on contending, in the most effective ways that present themselves, while it does remain possible.'

6 The War and Its Aftermath: Literature, Criticism and Education

The vitality of criticism must derive from the life of literature, and if *Scrutiny* deteriorated in the forties, the war was only the secondary reason. The main reason was that criticism in the thirties was still catching up with the literature of the twenties – a much livelier period than the thirties. As Leavis said,[1]

> The nineteen-twenties were the decade of Joyce, Eliot, D. H. Lawrence, Virginia Woolf, E. M. Forster, T. F. Powys, the effective publication of *Mauberley*, the discovery of Hopkins and the advent of Yeats as a major poet. The nineteen-thirties started with a Poetic Renascence. Now at their close one is driven to judge that the making accessible of Isaac Rosenberg (who has not yet been 'discovered', in spite of his great superiority in interest over Wilfrid Owen) was a more important event in English poetry than any emergence of a new poet.

Like *The Calendar of Modern Letters*, *Scrutiny* had been launched in a spirit of over-optimism about feedback. Surely a magazine that inculcated higher critical standards would be helping the creative writer by making the interested public more coherent and providing it with a forum for intelligent discussion. *Scrutiny* was more concerned than *The Calendar* was with the literature of the past, and, even in the thirties, it published much less creative work. Apart from posthumous work by Isaac Rosenberg, the only poetry to appear in *Scrutiny* was by Richard Eberhart, Ronald Bottrall, Selden Rodman, Don Luis de Gongora and C. H. Peacock. But the essays and reviews were far less negative and dismissive in their attitude to current writing than they became in the forties. Reviewing Orwell's *Inside the Whale* in 1940, Mrs Leavis conceded that he had 'grown up', unlike 'the nucleus of the literary world who christian-name each other and are in honour bound to advance each other's literary career'. She had read three or four of his novels and concluded 'if he would give up trying to be a novelist Mr Orwell might find his metier in literary

[1] 'Retrospect of a Decade', *Scrutiny* IX 1, June 1940.

criticism, in a special line of it peculiar to himself and which is particularly needed now. . . .' His new book suggested that 'though his
is not primarily a literary approach he is that rare thing, a non-
literary writer who is also sensitive to literature'. But when his
Critical Essays came out in 1946 they were welcomed rather briefly
by T. R. Barnes, who found his sensibility blunt in comparison with
Edmund Wilson's, and *Scrutiny* ignored both *Animal Farm* (1945) and
1984 (1949).

In December 1942 Mrs Leavis picked out Arthur Koestler's
Darkness at Noon as 'a novel to be most strongly recommended'. This
was her only recommendation during the forties and (except for a
letter in 1950 about *Sir Gawain and the Green Knight*) she wrote
nothing for *Scrutiny* after 1947. The burden had been too great. Since
it started in 1932 she had been the main authority on fiction, and she
had worked editorially on fiction reviews by other writers. Generally
there was little interference with contributors' work, though occa-
sionally reviewers would find the virginity of their review copies had
been violated by such marginal annotations as 'Meta-waffle' in
Leavis's handwriting.

Reviewing Dylan Thomas's stories *A Portrait of the Artist as a Young
Dog*, W. H. Mellers complained that his 'terrors and raptures and
desires' were identical with those of Dylan Thomas the child. 'His
writing then becomes pivoted on himself, an orgy of self-commisera-
tion.' Discussing *For Whom the Bell Tolls*, Mellers concluded that
Hemingway 'should restrict himself to short stories where the accuracy of his reporter's eye and his limitation of emotional range help
rather than hinder him'. When Virginia Woolf's *Between the Acts*
came out in 1941, soon after her suicide, Leavis's verdict was that
her only good novel had been *To the Lighthouse*. 'The preoccupation
with intimating "significance" in fine shades of consciousness,
together with the unremitting play of visual imagery, the "beautiful"
writing and the lack of moral interest and interest in action, give the
effect of something closely akin to a sophisticated aestheticism.'

Graham Greene's reputation went on growing throughout the
forties, but, except for a passing comment about French reactions to
his work, *Scrutiny* passed no judgment until 1952, when F. N. Lees
found it impossible 'to ignore the crude analysis, the obtrusive and
deforming emotionalism, and the defective presentational technique
which is at the least no aid in exploring and revealing the issues concerned'. Dylan Thomas's *Deaths and Entrances* received an extended

review from Wolf Mankowitz: 'Clever-boy pranks in verbal gym-
nastics are a rather touching tribute to the critics who have over a
period of some twenty years attempted to establish the seriousness
of poetry, but such exhibitions cannot be mistaken for seriousness
themselves.' Reviewing Thomas's *Collected Poems* in the issue dated
Winter 1952-3, Robin Mayhead found even more 'gross pretentious-
ness' in the later poems than in the early ones.

A 1951 review by Marius Bewley pricked at Christopher Fry's
ballooning reputation, and a critical exchange between D. W.
Harding and John Farrelly contributed towards a reassessment of
Scott Fitzgerald, but it cannot be claimed that the last two volumes
of *Scrutiny* did as much as the first nine to keep readers *au courant* with
important developments in the arts. Two of H. A. Mason's best pieces
for *Scrutiny* were about the early work of Sartre and Camus, but there
was no coverage of what either of them wrote from 1948 onwards.
Leavis had reviewed *Our Exagmination Round his Factification for Incam-
ination of Work in Progress* but failed to notice what Beckett went on
to write. The only reference to Robert Lowell, William Carlos
Williams or Wallace Stevens occurred in a review of B. Rajan's
Focus Number Five: Modern American Poetry by Marius Bewley who
devoted seven pages to Lowell and one to Stevens, mentioning
Williams only *en passant*. D. J. Enright wrote perceptively about
Thomas Mann, but no one raised the subject of Brecht.

When Leavis had first spoken to undergraduates about Lawrence
and Joyce, they were both still alive, and his enthusiasm for their
work provided energy to fuel all his excursions into the literary past.
When Eliot published *Little Gidding*, the last of his *Four Quartets*, in
1942, it was obvious to Leavis that great poetry was still being
written in England, and it was as necessary to make sure that it was
appreciated, at least by an educated minority, as to fight against the
inflation of Auden's and Spender's reputations. Throughout the
forties and early fifties it was also necessary to rescue D. H. Lawrence,
whose reputation had been badly damaged by critics who took their
cue from Eliot's sneer in *After Strange Gods* at 'his lack of sense
of humour, a certain snobbery, a lack not so much of information as
of the critical faculties which education should give, an incapacity for
what we ordinarily call thinking'. Leavis did more than anyone else
to win for Lawrence's books their present popularity, but Lawrence
was already dead.

Meanwhile *Scrutiny* had been damaged by the war, which not only removed many contributors and potential contributors from Cambridge, but made it harder to agitate for an educational revolution. Temporarily, at least, attitudes were pushed towards conservatism: the British people was fighting to keep what it had. Even in the English School at Cambridge, Leavis was still almost powerless. He was not invited to become a member of the Faculty Board until 1954, in spite of – or perhaps partly because of – the theoretical formulations and the excellent practical proposals that he offered between 1940 and 1943 in four *Scrutiny* essays under the title *Education and the University*[1]. In November of 1943 they were published as a book, with an appendix consisting of Leavis's review of Eliot's 'The Dry Salvages' and *How to Teach Reading*. In the second edition (1948) *Mass Civilization and Minority Culture* was added to the appendix.

By the seventies, of course, he had become less optimistic about education, but during the war he could say: 'It is still possible to believe that the obvious drift – or drive – of civilization doesn't exhaustively represent "the hopes, the knowledge, the values, the beliefs" of the society to which we belong. And it is in fact in that society conventionally assumed that education should be in some ways concerned with countering certain characteristic tendencies of civilization.' This statement was prompted by Alexander Meiklejohn's book *The Experimental College*[2], which had made the point that schools and colleges, being part of a social order, inculcate the same values, beliefs and so on. Leavis put forward a proposition which had a force almost contradictory to Dr Meiklejohn's: that education should 'preserve and develop a continuity of consciousness and a mature directing sense of value – a sense of value informed by a traditional wisdom'. Meiklejohn recognized that 'the drift of American life is against those forms of liberal thinking which seem most essential to its welfare'. Leavis knew that the war would accelerate the process of Americanizing Western Europe and that it was essential for a liberal education, free from religious or political premises, to cultivate the civilized values that were worth preserving. The claims he made for literary criticism as a useful discipline centred on the argument that: 'It trains, in a way no other discipline can, intelligence and sensibility together, cultivating a sensitiveness and precision of response and a delicate integrity of intelligence –

[1] *Scrutiny* IX 2, September 1940, IX 3, December 1940, IX 4, March 1941 and XI 3, Spring 1943.
[2] Harper, U.S.A. 1932.

intelligence that integrates as well as analyses and must have perti-
nacity and staying power as well as delicacy.' Discipline of thought
must at the same time be 'a discipline in scrupulous sensitiveness of
response to delicate organizations of feeling, sensation and imagery'.

Writing about the current situation at Cambridge, he was too
outspoken to win favour with those who could have given him more
power. He acknowledged that undergraduates derived less stimulus
from the formal teaching than from the friendships and the conversations that the ambiance encouraged. In each college students and
lecturers would find themselves living, eating and drinking at close
quarters with others who were involved in different subjects. Rich
opportunities were provided for discussion across the frontiers of
specialization but little was done to foster intra-departmental
communication.

Leavis went on to criticize the examination system. Candidates
were forced to depend on what they could 'scribble in three hours,
with journalistic facility and that athletic endurance which has
nothing to do with the qualities that should properly be tested'. It
would be better if they were also invited to submit reviews, written
in their own time, of recent fiction, verse and criticism. Altogether
there should be less emphasis on the examinations at the end of each
year and more on the individual work done in between. Generally,
undergraduates were not being given enough help in acquiring the
art of reading creatively. Aristotle, Longinus, Sidney, Dryden and
Addison were given too much space on the curriculum, and Dante
not enough.

Leavis's proposals were not put into practice, but the book was
an immediate success. After being published on 4 November, it was
reprinted before the end of the month. Meanwhile *New Bearings* was
in its third impression and *Culture and Environment* in its fourth. In
July 1945, when the Attlee government came to power, Leavis was
fifty. Suddenly the atmosphere was alive with prospects of reform.
The educational revolution Leavis wanted was as remote as ever,
but with the improvement in quantity and quality of the students
choosing to read English and with the possibility of co-ordinating
Leavis's courses with those of other Downing lecturers, it must have
seemed there was a genuine hope of realizing at least some of his
ambitions for an experimental college. There was also a new surge
of literary activity. Several new little reviews were founded, including
Humanitas, the *Cambridge Journal*, *Politics and Letters* and *Critic*. It even

seemed possible that Leavis and *Scrutiny* might be able to break through the conspiracy of Establishment silence. When *The Great Tradition* came out in 1948, the *Times Literary Supplement* devoted a whole middle page to a review written by a regular contributor to *Scrutiny*. But something went wrong. The progress was not consolidated. The reasons were complex. The Leavises had both taxed their reserves of physical, intellectual and emotional energy throughout the thirties and the war. Their domestic problems were exacerbated by illness and the needs of a young family. This wouldn't have mattered so much if Leavis had found co-editors and contributors to whom he could confidently have delegated more responsibility, but too much of the burden remained on his own tired shoulders, though *Scrutiny* was damaged less by personal exhaustion than by modification of its objectives. The theories and the practical proposals of *Education and the University* are equally admirable, but, unlike the pre-war articles in *Scrutiny*, they cannot be described as revolutionary.

7 Leavis and the Novel

'It is not for nothing,' Leavis had written in 1932,[1] 'that criticism of the novel has hardly yet begun.' Prose demands the same approach as verse, 'but admits it far less readily'. 'Everything that the novelist does is done with words' but his effects are less concentrated. He depends more on the accumulation that is taking place inside the reader's mind and, though the techniques of practical criticism can usefully be applied, it is impossible to sample the quality of the whole by isolating a passage.

C. H. Rickword, Edgell's cousin, had hit hard against conventional notions of character and story in two seminal notes on fiction in *The Calendar*. The quality of a novel depended on 'a unity among the events, a progressive rhythm that includes and reconciles each separate rhythm . . . the idea of a human being which is carried away from a play or a novel, is a product of the narrative . . . The technique of the novel is just as symphonic as the technique of the drama and as dependent, up to a point, on the dynamic devices of articulation and control of narrative tempo . . . More important, then, than what may be called the tricks of narrative is the status of plot and its relation to the other elements of a novel, particularly its relation to character, in solution.'

The point Rickword was making in calling the novel 'symphonic' was reinforced by Leavis in the phrase 'The Novel as Dramatic Poem', which he used as a title for a series of essays in *Scrutiny*. His approach, like Rickword's, was very different from the usual one, based on the assumption that the business of the novelist 'is to "create a world", and the mark of the master is external abundance – he gives you lots of "life". The test of life in his characters (he must above all create "living" characters) is that they go on living outside the book. Expectations as unexacting as these are not when they encounter significance, grateful for it, and when it meets them in that insistent form where nothing is very engaging as "life" unless its relevance is fully taken, miss it altogether.' *Hard Times*, like *The Europeans*, could be called a 'moral fable', by which Leavis meant that

[1] *How to Teach Reading.*

'in it the intention is peculiarly insistent, so that the representative significance of everything in the fable – character, episode, and so on – is immediately apparent as we read.'[1]

It was in 1936, after finishing his two books on poetry, that he turned his attention to the novel, which previously he had left to his wife. After *Fiction and the Reading Public* she had written several articles about fiction and reviews of novels for *Scrutiny*; during the war she would go on to write a series of four essays – totalling 93 pages – about Jane Austen, but she never completed another book except in collaboration with her husband. Apart from her writing and editorial work, she had three children to bring up, a house to run, food to cook and a series of serious illnesses which made the doctors forecast she had not long to live. When she could, she went on teaching for the university, though she was never offered so much as an assistant lectureship, but the essential work on the novel was left to be done by her husband. He had already written about Lawrence and briefly about Dickens and Dreiser. His next extended essay on a novelist was written for the *Scrutiny* that came out in March 1937, a twenty-page review of *The Art of the Novel*, Richard Blackmur's collection of Henry James's Critical Prefaces. They belong, as Leavis put it, to James's 'late, difficult period', and Leavis was critical of James's habit, in both novels and Prefaces, 'of presenting, of leaving presented, the essential thing by working round and behind so that it shapes itself in the space left amidst a context of hints and apprehensions'. This point cannot be substantiated without reference back to the earlier work: Leavis salutes *Washington Square* (1880), *The Portrait of a Lady* (1881) and *The Bostonians* (1886) 'which ought to be generally current classics; that they are not can only be due to the fact that we are all sent to the late difficult works first . . . all three have the abundant, full-blooded life of well-nourished organisms.' The essay ends by asking 'what achievement in the art of fiction – fiction as a completely serious art addressed to the adult mind – can we point to in English as surpassing his?'

Though it was written as a review of the collected prefaces, this essay became the second part of the critique on Henry James's novels in *The Great Tradition*. The two essays which make up the chapter on Conrad appeared in June and October 1941 (X 1 and 2), and the four on George Eliot in 1945–6: XIII 3, Autumn-Winter 1945; XIII

---

[1] 'The Novel as Dramatic Poem' (1): *Hard Times*, *Scrutiny* XIV 3, Spring 1947. This essay is reprinted both in *The Great Tradition* and in *Dickens the Novelist*.

4, Spring 1946; XIV 1, Summer 1946, and XIV 2, December 1946.
The first five appeared under the title 'Revaluations' and the essay
on Dickens's *Hard Times*, the first in the series 'The Novel as Dramatic
Poem' came out in XIV 3, Spring 1947). *The Great Tradition* was
published in 1948. Henry James's 'Daniel Deronda: a Conversation'
was printed after the *Hard Times* chapter as an Appendix.

Apart from the first section of the Henry James critique, the only
part of the book to be newly written was the introductory section,
'The Great Tradition'. It began: 'The great English novelists are
Jane Austen, George Eliot, Henry James and Joseph Conrad – to
stop for the moment at that comparatively safe point in history.
Since Jane Austen, for special reasons, needs to be studied at considerable length, I confine myself in this book to the last three.'

In a footnote on page 2 he blamed Virginia Woolf and E. M.
Forster for 'the fashion . . . of talking of *Moll Flanders* as a "great
novel"'. Defoe had mattered little as an influence, while Sterne had
been guilty of 'irresponsible (and nasty) trifling', which had been
overrated in the twenties and used as a 'sanction for attributing
value to other trifling'. Bunyan had been important in the history of
'the English-speaking consciousness'. 'His influence would tend
strongly to reinforce the un-Flaubertian quality of the line of English
classical fiction . . . as well as to co-operate with the Johnsonian
tradition of morally significant typicality in characters.' Fielding, he
said, 'deserves the place of importance given him in the literary
histories, but he hasn't the kind of classical distinction we are also
invited to credit him with. He is important not because he leads to
Mr J. B. Priestley but because he leads to Jane Austen, to appreciate
whose distinction is to feel that life isn't long enough to permit of
one's giving much time to Fielding or any to Mr Priestley. . . . There
can't be subtlety of organization without richer matter to organize,
and subtler interests, than Fielding has to offer.'

Richardson's *Clarissa* is 'a really impressive work. But it's no use
pretending that Richardson can ever be made a current classic
again. The substance of interest that he too has to offer is in its own
way extremely limited in range and variety, and the demand he
makes on the reader's time is in proportion – and absolutely – so
immense as to be found, in general, prohibitive (though I don't
know that I wouldn't sooner read through again *Clarissa* than *A la
recherche du temps perdu*).'

Besides being limited by Leavis's unwillingness to carry it further

forwards into the twentieth century, *The Great Tradition* is also handi-
capped by his refusal to concern himself with what he admits is 'one
of the important lines of English literary history – Richardson-Fanny
Burney – Jane Austen'. There is a footnote to advise the reader 'For
the relation of Jane Austen to other writers see the essay by Q. D.
Leavis, *A Critical Theory of Jane Austen's Writings*, in *Scrutiny*, Vol X,
No. I.' Leavis tells us explicitly that the first modern novelist is not
George Eliot but Jane Austen. Why then begin with George Eliot?
The book could have been as long as he wanted to make it, but Mrs
Leavis had already written so much about Jane Austen in *Scrutiny*
that he may have been unwilling to encroach on her territory, and
they had not yet started on the collaborative method they were to use
in *Lectures in America* (1969) and *Dickens the Novelist* (1970).

As it is, 'The Great Tradition' would have been a more appropriate title for *Revaluation* than for this book, which concentrates on a
trio that includes an American and a Pole whose second language was
French. When Leavis concedes that Conrad and Henry James were
greatly influenced by Dickens, his exclusion seems all the more
remarkable. Most readers would have expected him to be put in the
centre of the great tradition, but Leavis wrote: 'That Dickens was a
great genius and is permanently among the classics is certain. But the
genius was that of a great entertainer, and he had for the most part
no profounder responsibility as a creative artist than this description
suggests.' *Hard Times* was his only novel in which he left himself 'no
room for the usual repetitive overdoing and loose inclusiveness'.
Thackeray and Trollope were also excluded. They had 'nothing to
offer the reader whose demand goes beyond the "creation of characters" and so on'. More surprisingly Leavis concurred with Henry
James's patronizing dismissal of Hardy: 'The good little Thomas
Hardy has scored a great success with *Tess of the d'Urbervilles*, which is
chock-full of faults and falsity, and yet has a singular charm.' The
omission that seems to have caused Leavis most hesitation is that of
Emily Bronte. He respected her for breaking so resolutely 'both with
the Scott tradition that imposed on the novelist a romantic resolution
of his themes, and with the tradition coming down from the eighteenth
century that demanded a plane-mirror reflection of the surface of
"real" life'. But *Wuthering Heights* still struck him as 'a kind of sport'.
His wife, who took it more seriously, wrote extremely well about it in
Lectures in America. (Her essay is well over twice as long as the lecture
on which she based it.)

Conrad was the first novelist Leavis studied with the intention of writing a comprehensive critique. 'I read through his works with close attention, and pondered and compared and (where I felt the challenge) re-read, until I arrived at a clear understanding with myself as to what, as they impressed me, his distinction and his greatness were, and in what places they were most notably to be found.'[1] But the two resulting essays, which fill 55 pages of *The Great Tradition*, disregard a large proportion of Conrad's fiction, dismissing some of his most highly regarded novels, such as *Lord Jim*, very tersely. Both decisions are justifiable. Conrad's numerous potboilers are flabby and overwritten; *Lord Jim* is overrated. Leavis concentrates unerringly on the best work: *Nostromo, Typhoon, The Shadow-Line, Victory* and *The Secret Agent*. His comments are always perceptive and helpful, but they do not altogether vindicate the claim he makes in the later essay on Henry James which comes earlier in the book: that Conrad was

> a greater novelist than Flaubert because of the greater range and depth of his interest in humanity and the greater intensity of his moral preoccupation . . . to appreciate Conrad's 'form' is to take stock of a process of relative valuation conducted by him in the face of life: what do men live by? what can men live by? . . . The dramatic imagination at work is an intensely moral imagination, the vividness of which is inalienably a judging and a valuing.

Nor do they substantiate his argument that Conrad is 'more completely an artist' than George Eliot: 'he transmutes more completely into the created work the interests he brings in.' Though Leavis does succeed in demonstrating how the moral intensity enhances the vividness of the dramatization, he overstresses the 'Shakespearean' element in *Nostromo*; and though the final scene between Verloc and his wife in *The Secret Agent* is extremely powerful, surely it is not 'one of the most astonishing triumphs of genius in fiction'.

Taking the novels out of chronological order, Leavis never recognizes one of the main failures in Conrad's development as an artist: his inability to build on his own previous achievement. *Nostromo* (1904) should have been of more help to the fiction of the next thirteen years. Greater success might have brought him more self-confidence as an artist; lacking it, he tended to start almost from

---

[1] 'Joseph Conrad' in the *Sewanee Review* April–June 1958, reprinted in *Anna Karenina and Other Essays* under the title 'The Shadow-Line'.

scratch each time. He was also more of a romantic than the Conrad who emerges from Leavis's critique. As Frank Kermode has put it,[1] for him art was 'not to do with wisdom but with the obscure emotional satisfaction of finding meaning in catastrophe, moments of sense in the barren fury of human behaviour'. But when he attained belatedly to commercial success, he attributed it to his faith in 'the solidarity of all mankind in simple ideas and sincere emotions'. Leavis concedes that he was 'in some respects a simple soul', pointing to the lack of irony and the Poe-like melodramatic intensities in *Heart of Darkness*. He also draws attention to the intrusiveness of the recurrent adjectives 'inscrutable', 'inconceivable', 'unspeakable', which are 'applied to the evocation of human profundities and spiritual horrors; to magnifying a thrilled sense of the unspeakable potentialities of the human soul'. But on the whole Leavis is surprisingly tolerant of the rhetoric Conrad so often used when, he could not trust the facts of his fiction to speak for themselves. As he said in a letter to David Meldrum apropos his character Falk, 'I wanted to make him stand for so much that I neglected, in a manner, to set him on his feet.'

His best novel was *Nostromo*, and the 11 pages Leavis devotes to it constitute the best part of his critique. As he says, each character and situation is given its significance so economically in such a 'taut inclusive scheme', that the novel has a better claim to the description 'moralized fable' than any fiction of George Eliot's except *Silas Marner*. The main public or political theme is the relation between moral idealism and material interests, while the private themes all have a representative moral significance. The book's impressiveness depends more on this than on 'any profundity of search into human experience, or any explorative subtlety in the analysis of human behaviour'. Conrad's central preoccupation is with 'the relation between the material and the spiritual'. As he said himself, 'All my concern has been with the "ideal" value of things, events and people.' That is arguably more of a limitation in a twentieth-century novelist than Leavis acknowledges, and though he points to a hollowness at the centre of *Nostromo*, he holds back from attributing it to the disparity (which he diagnoses correctly) between the radical scepticism of Martin Decoud, whose consciousness permeates and dominates the novel, and the romantic inclinations of an author temperament-

[1] Reviewing Jocelyn Baines's biography of Conrad in *The Spectator*, 5 February 1960.

ally attracted to the characters capable of 'investing their activities with spiritual value'.

It was four years later, in his four essays on George Eliot, that Leavis attained to maturity as a critic of the novel. He was fortunate in being able to look over the shoulders of Henry James, who had not only written the best criticism then in existence of her work but been influenced by it in his own practice as a novelist. One reason for the superiority of the George Eliot critique over the Conrad is that Leavis, having now digested more of Henry James's fiction criticism, is more aware of how important it is to base a narrative on an adequate centre of consciousness. Discussing *Madame Bovary* James had asked:[1]

> Why did Flaubert choose, as special conduits of the life he proposed to depict, such inferior and in the case of Frederic such abject human specimens? . . . He wished in each case to make a picture of experience – middling experience, it is true – and of the world close to him; but if he imagined nothing better for his purpose than such a heroine and such a hero, both such limited reflectors and registers, we are forced to believe it to have been by a defect of his mind. And that sign of weakness remains even if it be objected that the images in question were addressed to his purpose better than others would have been: the purpose itself then shows as inferior.

James was equally critical of Balzac's preoccupation with the small change of material existence: he called him 'a man of business doubled with an artist'. If Leavis tilts in passing at both Flaubert and Balzac, it is because he shares James's attitude, but he does not accept the antithesis James proposes in his criticism of George Eliot[2]: for her, the novel 'was not primarily a picture of life, capable of deriving a high value from its form, but a moralized fable, the last word of a philosophy endeavouring to teach by example.' Her 'figures and situations', he objects, are 'not *seen* in the irresponsible plastic way'. But, as Leavis ripostes, 'Is there any great novelist whose preoccupation with "form" is not a matter of his responsibility towards a rich human interest, or complexity of interests, profoundly realized? – a responsibility involving, of its very nature, imaginative sympathy, moral discrimination and judgment of relative human value?'

James's generalization about George Eliot is inadequate: 'She

---

[1] This is quoted by Andor Gomme in *Attitudes to Criticism*. Southern Illinois University Press 1966.
[2] In *Partial Portraits*.

proceeds from the abstract to the concrete . . . her figures and situations are evolved . . . from the moral consciousness and are only
indirectly the products of observation.' Though he departs from the
conventional view of her work in defending parts of *Daniel Deronda*,
he inclines to support the notion then prevalent that her talent was at
its best in *Scenes of Clerical Life, Adam Bede, The Mill on the Floss* and
Silas Marner; that it declined as she used up her memories of her own
childhood and youth, coming to rely more on her formidable intellectual powers. But Leavis bases his main claim for her on *Middlemarch*
and the parts of *Daniel Deronda* that deal with Gwendolen Harleth and
Grandcourt.

He is not intolerant towards the early work, but he is embarrassed
by 'an emotional quality, one to which there is no equivalent in Jane
Austen'. The presence of George Eliot's own emotional needs is too
direct. In *Adam Bede* rustic life is presented more convincingly than in
Hardy's novels, but Adam is the Ideal Craftsman embodying the
Dignity of Labour. In a later essay[1] Leavis emphasizes the Wordsworthian element in Adam. 'We think of Michael.' The love story
fails to justify the space she gives it. 'There is not at work in the whole
any pressure from her profounder experience to compel an inevitable
development.'

The Mill on the Floss is better. In the autobiographical part there is
'the fresh directness of a child's vision', and it is good that 'the
creative powers at work here owe their successes as much to a very
fine intelligence as to powers of feeling and remembering'. But the
autobiographical element produces an over-emotional tone. 'We feel
an urgency, a resonance, a personal vibration, adverting us of the
poignantly immediate presence of the author.' The book glows with
the pleasure of an unattractive woman in imagining herself as a
beautiful child, and the 'soulful side of Maggie' is presented by
George Eliot with self-idealization, self-pity and a remarkable absence
of criticism. Barbara Hardy takes the opposite view, arguing[2] that
the book is 'very carefully critical of Maggie, both in direct commentary and through the voice of Philip: it criticizes Maggie's shift
from one dream to another, it criticizes her religiosity and her lack of
self-knowledge. Where it is indulgent – and I think it is "indulgent"
and not "self-indulgent" – it is in pitying while it criticizes, in pour-

[1] Written as a Foreword to the Signet edition of *Adam Bede*, New York 1961 and
reprinted in *Anna Karenina and Other Essays*.
[2] *Sphere History of English Literature* Vol. 6, 1969.

ing over Maggie, or Mr Tulliver, or Philip, in a constant flowing of love, knowing and maternal.'

Leavis has nothing but praise for the handling of Maggie's capitulation to her lover. Exhausted by the struggle, she 'surrenders to the chance that leaves her to embark alone with Stephen, and then, with inert will, lets the boat carry her down-stream until it is too late, so that the choice seems taken from her'. Professor Hardy finds the novel 'indulgent in the resolution by plot, the restoration of the dream of childhood, relationship, and total understanding in the flood'.

Leavis attributes the success of *Silas Marner* to 'the absence of personal immediacy'. The mood is of 'enchanted adult reminiscence'. He compares its 'charm' unfavourably with the 'heightened reality' of Dickens's *Hard Times*. Nor has he much to say in defence of *Romola*, which derives from literary research, with another idealized version of the authoress as heroine. But, discussing *Felix Holt*, he praises the dialogue between Jermyn and Mrs Transome as 'astonishingly finer and maturer than anything George Eliot had done before . . . the perceiving focuses the profound experience of years – experience worked over by reflective thought, and so made capable of focusing.' Instead of being 'worsted by emotional needs', her 'magnificent intelligence' was functioning as 'mature understanding'.

In *Felix Holt* she asserts that 'there is no private life which has not been determined by a wider public life'; in *Middlemarch* she substantiates the assertion. Virginia Woolf called it 'one of the few English novels written for grown-up people'; Leavis calls it the only book which *as a whole* represents George Eliot's mature genius. He applauds her treatment of Casauban and her understanding of Lydgate. She admires his intellectual idealism without ennobling his martyrdom to Rosamond's femininity, which is incapable of either idealism or intellectual interests. But George Eliot shows that, as a lover, he is complementary to her: 'he held it one of the prettiest attributes of the feminine mind to adore a man's pre-eminence without too precise a knowledge of what it consisted in.' George Eliot has little sympathy for Rosamond but criticizes her with deadly accuracy: 'She was by nature an actress of parts that entered into her *physique*: she even acted her own character, and so well, that she did not know it to be precisely her own.'

But there is one disconcerting 'enclave of the old immaturity' in the book. Dorothea 'is a product of George Eliot's own "soul-hunger" –

another day-dream ideal self'. Leavis deploys lengthy quotations very subtly to demonstrate the lack of poise in George Eliot's treatment of her heroine. Will Ladislaw's attitude to her is indistinguishable from the writer's, while 'the situations offered by way of "objective correlative" have the day-dream relation to experience; they are generated by a need to soar above the indocile facts and conditions of the real world. They don't, indeed, strike us as real in any sense; they have no objectivity, no vigour of illusion.'

Barbara Hardy again quarrels[1] with Leavis's strictures against the heroine. She concedes that George Eliot abruptly withdraws her irony when she comes to Dorothea's relationship with Will. 'But irony is not the only corrective to excessive sympathy and pathos, and George Eliot's reflective tone acts throughout the novel as a strong corrective, even when it is used at the same time as a sentimental image.' Yes, but it is not strong enough to scale down Dorothea's image of herself as Gwendolen Harleth's is scaled down by the confrontation with Klesmer, the musician who makes her recognize the absurdity of her ambition to embark on a musical career.

Like *Middlemarch*, *Daniel Deronda* has a double plot, and Leavis almost ignores 'the bad half', which concerns Deronda; he is preoccupied with showing how previous critics had concentrated on this half, approving of George Eliot without appreciating her real strength and distinction, which can best be seen in the good half. If this could be extricated for separate publication, he maintains it would be not only a self-sufficient whole but a great novel. He even proposes a title for it – *Gwendolen Harleth*. When a publisher invited him to do the work of extrication himself, he rose to the challenge, but *Gwendolen Harleth* never appeared in the bookshops, so his theory has not been put to the ultimate test.

Leavis is cogent in his argument that if Henry James had not read *Daniel Deronda*, he would not have written *The Portrait of a Lady*. Even if James's novel is inferior to 'the good half' of George Eliot's, this is too indirect a suggestion of its quality for the reader who has not yet come to the chapter on *Henry James*. Leavis's elaborate comparison was more acceptable as an essay in *Scrutiny* than as a chapter in a book on the novel.

His reluctance to rewrite has an even more debilitating effect on his Henry James chapter. Unlike the component essays in *Revaluation*,

[1] *The Novels of George Eliot*. Athlone Press 1959.

the review of James's collected prefaces had not been written with the intention that it would eventually be integrated into a book; the new half of the chapter is titled 'To The Portrait of a Lady', so the climacteric subject is partly exhausted before the chapter is even begun. While the backbone of the George Eliot critique is chronological, the Henry James, which has a very crooked spine, gives the reader less help towards forming a clear impression of his development as a novelist. Reviewing the prefaces, Leavis was at pains to show that James had become a writer so very different from the author of his early books that he shouldn't even be taken as a critical authority on them. The argument of Edmund Wilson's essay 'The Ambiguity of Henry James' is summarized: 'as the later manner developed, the subtleties of James's technique, the inexplicitnesses and indirections of his methods of presentment, tended to subserve a fundamental ambiguity; one, that is, about which he was not himself clear.' Leavis accepts Wilson's suggestion that the confusion had its roots in an internal dispute between American and European viewpoints. The over-subtlety of the late novels and the 'loss of sureness in his moral touch' are closely connected. *The Ambassadors*, 'which he seems to have thought his greatest success, produces an effect of disproportionate "doing" – of a technique the subtleties and elaborations of which are not sufficiently controlled by a feeling for value and significance in living. What, we ask, is this, symbolized by Paris, that Strether feels himself to have missed in his own life? Has James himself sufficiently inquired? Is it anything adequately realized?'

Unsatisfactory as Leavis's chapter is, it exerted a useful influence towards achieving a consensus that James was at his best not in *The Wings of the Dove* (1902) *The Ambassadors* (1903) and *The Golden Bowl* (1905) but in the period of his early maturity from *Washington Square* and *The Portrait of a Lady* (both 1881) to *The Bostonians* (1886). Leavis also puts a high valuation on *What Maisie Knew* (1897) and *The Awkward Age* (1899), the two novels which came after the hiatus in the early nineties when James was writing unsuccessfully for the theatre. If his fiction deteriorated after the turn of the century, it was not simply a matter of losing touch with his memories of America. As Leavis says, 'being a novelist came to be too large a part of his living; that is, he did not live enough. . . . Essentially he was in quest of an ideal society, an ideal civilization. And English society, he had to recognize as he lived into it, could not after all offer him any sustaining approximation to his ideal.' He was also driven back on

himself by the realization that his art could appeal only to a tiny
minority.

Both halves of Leavis's chapter make excellent points. He defends
The Awkward Age against Edmund Wilson's strictures; he shows that
from understanding how much there was to learn from Jane Austen
and George Eliot, James came to realize how little he needed from the
French masters; there is a comparison of *Washington Square* with
Balzac's *Eugénie Grandet* and an analysis of Dickens's influence on
Roderick Hudson: James was helped 'to see from the outside, and
critically place, the life around him'. But Leavis keeps circling
around the same points.

I think he is right to see *The Portrait of a Lady* as central to James's
achievement, and his criticism of it is most judicious. 'Convincingly
"there" as scene and persons are, and though the imagination that
makes them so present to us is ironically perspicacious and supremely
intelligent, there is something of James's ideal civilization about the
England he evokes.' There is also some idealization in the attempt to
establish the supremacy of the American girl. 'Her freedom in the
face of English conventions appears – and she is a firmly realized
presence for us – as a true emancipation of spirit. Unlike Daisy
Miller she has her own superior code, in her scruple, her self-respect
and her sensitiveness; she is educated and highly intelligent.' Her
American admirer, Caspar Goodwood, is less firmly realized,
because he is sentimentalized. Without minimizing the novel's
defects and in spite of having to return to it three times instead of
assimilating the end of the George Eliot essay and the review of the
Prefaces into a chronological treatment of Henry James, Leavis
vindicates the high claim he made for *The Portrait of a Lady*, rescuing
it from the neglect it had been suffering.

Richly though *The Great Tradition* deserves its reputation as one of
the best books ever written on the English novel, it could have been
far better if, instead of reprinting so many of his essays, Leavis had
taken time to throw the material back into the melting pot and forge
something new.

8   Leavis and the Critical Tradition

The problem Leavis presented to his publishers was not simple. To serve him well would have been extremely difficult because it would have involved mastering him, at least to the extent of overcoming his resistance to writing new material and rewriting old material. Despite the effectiveness of his books in penetrating to a much wider audience than he could reach as a lecturer or editor, his inclination was to go on regarding them as a by-product of the work that remained centred on Cambridge. He was still a slow writer who in practice had to give priority to lectures, seminars and editing *Scrutiny*, and in principle was concerned primarily to go on doing everything he could towards realizing his idea of a university. Perhaps there was a strong unconscious revulsion from the idea of a wide public. In any case the communication at which he excelled involved an intimacy which could be stretched beyond the confines of a lecture-hall to the readership of a small magazine, but no further.

The Common Pursuit, which appeared in 1952, four years after *The Great Tradition*, was an unstructured collection of 24 essays by him which had mostly been published in *Scrutiny*. The earliest was 'The Irony of Swift', which had made its first appearance in March 1934 and already been reprinted in *Determinations*; the latest, on 'Mr Eliot and Milton', had been published in the *Sewanee Review* at the end of 1949. Some of the essays were on individual writers – Shakespeare, Milton, Pope, Johnson, Bunyan, Gerard Manley Hopkins, Henry James, Lawrence, T. S. Eliot, E. M. Forster – some on such general topics as 'Literature and Society' and the current cultural situation. The essays are arranged neither in the order Leavis wrote them nor according to the chronology of the subject matter. Some are dated, some not. 'Literature and Society', the substance of an address given to the London School of Economics Students' Union, is left undated even though it opens with the words 'Two or three years back'. If you look it up in *Scrutiny*, you find it was already ten years old when the book came out. Book reviews are not usually identified as such, and it is seldom clear which books were under review. In 'Johnson and Augustanism', originally a book review written for *The Kenyon Review*, the editor has not even troubled to cut the second sentence: 'I had better add at once that I write in England and as an Englishman.' Many of the titles are either misleading (like 'Sociology and Literature' and 'Henry James and the Function of Criticism') or cryptic (like 'The Logic of Christian Discrimination'). The book under review, Brother George Every's *Poetry and Personal Responsibility*, is of little interest today. Like D. H. Lawrence, Leavis is a reviewer who can invariably make worthwhile points in discussing a bad book, but the selection of material for *The Common Pursuit* is unforgivable. During the twenty years of *Scrutiny*'s existence Leavis had made over 120 contributions. Some of the essays in *The Common Pursuit* are among his best, while others are among the least worth preserving.

The editorial inefficiency and ineffectuality are bad enough, but what matters more is that a superb opportunity was missed of publishing a smaller collection with a discernible principle of relevance. Each essay would then illuminate the others. It might have been possible to persuade him into writing a few more Shakespearean essays to complement the four which appear in *The Common Pursuit* and the comparison of *Antony and Cleopatra* with Dryden's *All for Love*, which was published in *Scrutiny* V 2, September 1936, not to be reprinted in a book until nearly forty years later. Another interesting possibility would have been implicitly to define his place in the critical tradition by collecting his essays on the criticism of Coleridge, Dr Johnson, Matthew Arnold, T. S. Eliot and D. H. Lawrence. The essay on 'Johnson as Critic' (*Scrutiny* XII 3, Summer 1944) is excluded from *The Common Pursuit*, presumably because it overlaps at a few points with 'Johnson and Augustanism'. Judicious editing could have pruned the repetition and it would have been convenient for the reader to have both essays in the same volume. 'Johnson as Critic' was not reprinted until *Anna Karenina and Other Essays* came out in 1967, with the overlapping still unremedied.

T. S. Eliot had called Arnold 'rather a propagandist for criticism than a critic'[1]; Leavis found it impossible to read his essay on 'The Study of Poetry' without recognizing 'that we have to do with an extraordinarily distinguished mind in complete possession of its purpose and pursuing it with easy mastery – that, in fact, we are reading a great critic.' Arnold's description of poetry as 'criticism of life' should be taken not as a definition but as a reminder 'of the

[1] 'Arnold as Critic' in *Scrutiny* VII 3, December 1938.

nature of the criteria by which comparative judgments are made'. Here is Leavis's gloss on Arnold's intention:

> We make . . . our major judgments about poetry by bringing to bear the completest and profoundest sense of relative value that, aided by the work judged, we can focus from our total experience of life (which includes literature), and our judgment has intimate bearings on the most serious choices we have to make thereafter in our living.

For Eliot, 'The best of Arnold's criticism is an illustration of his ethical views.' But to Arnold, as Leavis points out, 'the evaluation of poetry as "criticism of life" is inseparable from its evaluation as poetry . . . the moral judgment that concerns us as critics must be at the same time a delicately relevant response of sensibility'. The 'high seriousness which comes from absolute sincerity' was an essential precondition both for poetic truth and poetic beauty. 'The superior character of truth and seriousness, in the matter and substance of the best poetry, is inseparable from the superiority of diction and manner marking its style and movement.'

Without claiming classic status for any of the other essays in the volume titled 'The Study of Poetry', Leavis applauds Arnold's placing of the great Romantics in order of merit: Wordsworth, Byron, Keats and Shelley. He also admires Arnold 'as a thinker about the problems of culture and society'[1]. He was fortunate in having a large and influential public capable of appreciating his categorization of his countrymen into Barbarians, Philistines and Populace: had the diagnosis been altogether justified it would have been altogether ignored. But if he had been more preoccupied with consistency and systematic thinking, he might have given less play to his virtues: 'the peculiar sensitive mobility of intelligence, the constantly fresh concern for a delicate apprehension of actualities, the lack of interest in merely theoretical conclusions and results.'

Leavis's verdict on Coleridge[2] was that 'He was very much more brilliantly gifted than Arnold, but nothing of his deserves the classical status of Arnold's best work.' His achievement as a critic was incommensurate with the quality of his mind. His famous description of the imagination in Chapter XIV of *Biographia Literaria* 'has more often, perhaps, caused an excited sense of enlightenment than it has led to improved critical practice or understanding'. He also failed to make

[1] Review of Lionel Trilling's *Matthew Arnold* in *Scrutiny* VIII 1, June 1939.
[2] 'Coleridge in Criticism' in *Scrutiny* IX 1, June 1940.

much practical use of the equally famous contrast he drew between Imagination and Fancy. 'The distinction as he illustrates it is a way of calling attention to the organic complexities of verbal life, meta-phorical and other, in which Imagination manifests itself locally: Fancy is merely an ancillary concept.'

But he did have a gift for critical analysis and he did play a major part in discrediting 'the external mechanical approach of the Neo-classic eighteenth century'. Coleridge was less critical than Arnold about the notion of poetry as the product of inspiration, but more reasonable than Shelley. It was a pity that Coleridge's account of the creative process did not have more influence on the development of Romanticism in the nineteenth century. His importance in the critical tradition depends less on influence than on his 'capacity for a kind of sensitive analytic penetration such as will hardly be found in any earlier critic'. Taken together, his writings on Shakespeare are disap-pointingly insubstantial, and even his observations about Wordsworth fail to coagulate into a solid critical corpus, though he sometimes arrived at important insights about rhythm, metre and diction. Cursed with excessive fluency in thinking, talking and writing, he never needed either to sharpen his ideas or to sustain them under the discipline of internal pressure within a careful structure. On the other hand, it was an advantage that his critical 'principles' were evolved out of practical criticism. His main critical successes were local and incidental, as when he effectively defined the element of 'wit' in Shakespeare's *Venus and Adonis*:

> You seem to be told nothing but to see and hear everything. Hence it is, that from the perpetual activity of attention required on the part of the reader; from the rapid flow, the quick change, and the playful nature of the thoughts and images; and above all from the alienation, and, if I may hazard such an expression, the utter *aloofness* of the poet's own feelings from those of which he is at once the painter and the analyst; that though the very subject cannot but detract from the pleasure of a delicate mind, yet never was poem less dangerous on a moral account.

Dr Johnson was incapable of Coleridge's psychological subtlety. 'But it can be said that Johnson, with his rational vigour and the directness of his appeal to experience, represents the best that criticism can do before Coleridge.' He was also 'a better critic of eighteenth-century poetry than Matthew Arnold'.[1] As in his treat-ment of Arnold nearly six years earlier, Leavis lays great stress on 'the

[1] 'Johnson as Critic' in *Scrutiny* XII 3, Summer 1944.

wards sex . . . Lawrence's preoccupation with sex seems to us much
less fairly to be called "obsession" than Mr Eliot's, and very much
preferable.'

Leavis continues the argument in his review of Eliot's *After Strange
Gods: a Primer of Modern Heresy*.[1] Eliot's attitudes 'to sex have been, in
prose and poetry, almost uniformly negative – attitudes of distaste,
disgust and rejection'. Whereas Lawrence was justified in his claim: 'I
always labour at the same thing, to make the sex relation valid and
precious, not shameful.' 'And who can question,' asks Leavis, 'that
something as different as this from Mr Eliot's bent in the matter is
necessary if the struggle to "re-establish a vital connection between
the individual and the race" is to mean anything?'

The phrase comes from *After Strange Gods*, which defines tradition
as 'the means by which the vitality of the past enriches the life of the
present'. This is in line with Eliot's 1919 essay 'Tradition and the
Individual Talent', which made two pronouncements which have
become famous: 'Poetry is not a turning loose of emotion, but an
escape from emotion; it is not the expression of personality, but an
escape from personality,' and 'The more perfect the artist, the more
completely separate in him will be the man who suffers and the mind
which creates.' Eliot's tone and rhythm are dignified and attractive:
like many others, Leavis was slow to apprehend the dangers in his
theory of impersonality. Lawrence has been quick to attack the
essay: 'This classiosity is bunkum; still more cowardice.' But Leavis's
criticism had deep roots in Eliot's idea of tradition, and it was not
until 1958[2] that Leavis dismissed the essay as 'notable for its ambigui-
ties, its logical inconsequences, its pseudo-precisions, its fallacious-
ness, and the aplomb of its equivocations and its specious cogency.'
Eliot's theory was insidiously designed to suggest that great art can be
created 'without the distinguished individual, distinguished by reason
of his potency as a conduit of urgent life and by the profound and
sensitive responsibility he gives proof of towards his living experience.'
With great writers, as Leavis insists, 'we don't find ourselves impelled
to think of the pressure of the artistic process as something apart from
the pressure of the living – the living life and the lived experience –
out of which the work has issued . . . An intensity of art devoted to

---

[1] 'Mr Eliot, Mr Wyndham Lewis and Lawrence' in *Scrutiny* III 2, September
1934. This is reprinted in *The Common Pursuit* under the same title but without
making it clear that it was written as a review of *After Strange Gods*.
[2] 'T. S. Eliot as Critic' in *Commentary*, New York November 1958.

expressing disgust at *la platitude bourgeoise* – Flaubert's opposing art to life as something apart from and superior to it – entails a self-contradiction; it portends an inner thwarting disorder, a profound vital disharmony that has defeated intelligence in the artist and made any but a strained and starved creativity impossible, 'In 1966[1] Leavis denounced the essay as 'an attempt to absolve the artist from responsibility towards life'. According to the essay, 'The effect of a work of art upon the person who enjoys it is an experience different in kind from any experience not of art.'

But he was a great critic in spite of his beliefs about the relationship between life and literature. Writing in 1947[2], Leavis describes his own debt to *The Sacred Wood*, Eliot's 1919 volume of essays which included 'Tradition and the Individual Talent': 'it was a matter of having had incisively demonstrated, for pattern and incitement, what the disinterested and effective application of intelligence to literature looks like, what is the nature of purity of interest, and what is meant by the principle (as Mr Eliot himself states it) that "when you judge poetry it is as poetry you must judge it, and not as another thing".' The best of his critical writings 'represent more powerfully and incisively the idea of literary criticism as a discipline – a special discipline of intelligence – than the work of any other critic in the language (or any in French that I know).' But in his later criticism Eliot is less closely engaged: 'the critic seems to me to have mis-applied his dangerous gift of subtle statement to the development of a manner (it is surprisingly suggestive in places of G. K. Chesterton) that gainsays the very purpose of criticism, and to have done so because of a radical uncertainty about his intention and its validity.'

In this essay Leavis argues that Lawrence 'is not to be accounted anything like as important in literary criticism as T. S. Eliot', even if his judgment is sounder. Reviewing *Phoenix* in 1937[3] Leavis had called Lawrence 'the finest literary critic of our time – a great literary critic if ever there was one . . . in purity of interest and sureness of self-knowledge he seems to me to surpass Mr Eliot.' Leavis was later to revert to this view. In 1969[4] he called Lawrence 'an incomparably

---

[1] 'Eliot's Classical Standing', printed in *Lectures in America*.
[2] 'Approaches to T. S. Eliot' in *Scrutiny* XV 1, December 1947. Reprinted in *The Common Pursuit*.
[3] 'The Wild Untutored Phoenix' in *Scrutiny* VI 3, December 1937. Reprinted in *The Common Pursuit*.
[4] 'English, Unrest and Continuity'. Reprinted in *Nor Shall My Sword*.

greater critic than Eliot'. He may have lacked Eliot's erudition but it was nonsensical to accuse him of 'an incapacity for what we ordinarily call thinking'.[1] Leavis defends the 'genius' apparent in the 'persistent integrity' of his early exploration of Hardy. He was 'intelligent as only the completely serious and disinterested can be' and 'his critical poise is manifested in . . . a lively ironic humour – a humour that for all its clear-sighted and mocking vivacity is quite without animus. For, idiosyncratic as Lawrence's style is, it would be difficult to find one more radically free from egotism.' In short, unlike Eliot, he can be proclaimed as a 'representative of health and sanity'.

[1] See page 63.

9 Practical Criticism

The bad critic stands between the reader and the text; the mediation of a good critic always encourages as much intimacy as the text warrants. All good criticism is practical in this sense, whether W. B. Yeats's achievement is being summed up in two pages, or twenty are being devoted to the analysis of a single sonnet. Necrophilia must be discouraged and when the language is dead or cancerous with cliché, the responsible critic must advise his readers, 'Don't waste time on it'; when it is alive and healthy, good criticism can stimulate us to come more closely and more creatively to grips with it, responding to a movement here, a poised ambiguity there. The good critic is both go-between and midwife, assisting at the realization of the life latent in the printed words.

In the mid-forties Leavis was intending to write a book on 'Judgment and Analysis'. Two extracts from his draft appeared in *Scrutiny* XIII but 'the will to carry out the original plan was not as strong as it had once been, and . . . what had been growing was my sense that the proper continuation of "Judgment and Analysis" – for the kind of illustrative demonstration printed in *Scrutiny* could hardly be "completed" – was actually represented by "extended criticism", of which, in great diversity, there was so much asking to be done.'[1] Another reason may have been that this sort of analytical work can be done more effectively in a lecture or seminar than in a book. Much depended on Leavis's management of his voice – on his tone, his timing, his inflections. A certain amount depended on the reaction of the audience to the life he was releasing from the anonymous passages of verse and prose on the sheets he had distributed.

If the situation was essentially theatrical, this was apt, because Leavis's idea of the way language should function is essentially dramatic. In Donne and Keats, no less than in Shakespeare, a pause imposed on the speaking voice by the end of a verse line, can be an 'analogical enactment' of the movement described:

[1] *The Living Principle*. This contains longer extracts from the unfinished book.

> On a huge hill,
> Cragged, and steep, truth stands, and hee that will
> Reach her, about must, and about must goe;
>   *   *   *   *
> And sometimes like a gleaner thou dost keep
> Steady thy laden head across a brook . . .

These are two illustrations Leavis offers[1] 'of a pervasive action of the verse – or action in the reader as he follows the verse: as he takes the meaning, re-creates the organization, responds to the play of the sense-movement against the verse structure, makes the succession of efforts necessary to pronounce the organized words, he performs in various modes a continuous analogical enactment'. The principles that Leavis applies in his Practical Criticism are deeply rooted in Johnson, Coleridge, Arnold, Eliot and Lawrence, and in his reactions to them. It is worth comparing the remarks of his I have just quoted with the quotation from Coleridge on p. 82. Though *Venus and Adonis* is not a play, the verse is highly dramatic in that the poet does not appear to be making statements but communicating a series of actions which produce quick changes in the reader's mind.

Four of the five passages of Practical Criticism in *The Living Principle* originally appeared in *Scrutiny*, and the one which is printed last in the book appeared first in the quarterly. It is a comparison of Shakespeare's *Antony and Cleopatra* with Dryden's version, *All for Love*.[2] Leavis had been provoked by Bonamy Dobrée's Introduction to the World's Classics volume of *Restoration Tragedies*. It called *All for Love* a 'proud and lovely masterpiece', conceding that Shakespeare's play 'contains finer poetry' but claiming that 'Dryden's has a more tragic effect'.

Leavis is easily able to demonstrate that Shakespeare's verse is more alive – superior in concreteness, variety and sensitiveness.

> Shakespeare's verse seems to enact its meaning, to do and to give rather than to talk about, whereas Dryden's is merely descriptive eloquence. The characteristic Shakespearean life asserts itself in Enobarbus's opening lines.
>
> > The barge she sat in, like a burnish'd throne,
> > Burn'd on the water . . .
>
> – The assonantal sequence, 'barge' – 'burnish'd' – 'burn'd', is alien in spirit to Dryden's handling of the medium (it reminds us of Hopkins

[1] 'Imagery and Movement' in *The Living Principle*.
[2] *Scrutiny* V 2, September 1936.

who, though he has a technical deliberateness of his own, is, in his use of English, essentially Shakespearean). The effect is to give the metaphor 'burn'd' a vigour of sensuous realization that it wouldn't otherwise have had; the force of 'burn' is reflected back through 'burnish'd' (felt now as 'burning' too) upon 'barge', so that the barge takes fire, as it were, before our eyes: we are much more than merely told that the barge 'burn'd'.

(The comparison with Hopkins has its point, though Leavis might have done better to look back at the enlivening alliteration and assonance in such fourteenth-century poems as *Sir Gawain and the Green Knight*, which must have affected Shakespeare.)

If substantiation were needed for Leavis's anti-Pound argument that imagery is not entirely visual[1], it would be provided by his analysis of Enobarbus's lines

> the silken tackle
> Swell with the touches of those flower-soft hands,
> That yarely frame the office.

'The hard and energetic associations of "tackle" (they are not overtly felt as such, but are transformed, as it were, into their opposite) give the adjective "silken" a strength of sensuous evocation that it would not otherwise have had. "Tackle" here, no doubt, is inclusive, and it is the sails that swell; so that to feel, as I have done (and do still), that the verb makes the reader's hand grasp and compress the silken rope was perhaps a mere private vagary. Yet the "touches" insist that "tackle" (to which they are drawn by alliteration) also includes here what it ordinarily denotes – hands take hold of cordage, and it seems impossible to dissociate "swell" from the tactual effect.'

Another good point of comparison is that, unlike Shakespeare's Antony, Dryden's 'couldn't have sat in the market-place whistling to the air; his dignity wouldn't have permitted it'. Dryden's 'tragic personae exist only in a world of stage-postures; decorum gone, everything is gone. . . . The emotion doesn't emerge from a given situation realized in its concrete particularity; it is stated, not presented or enacted. The explicitness is of the kind that betrays absence of realization.'

This 'critical exercise' was presumably written before Leavis started planning his book on 'Judgment and Analysis'. The extracts

[1] See pages 32–3.

published in 1945 apply the same principles, once again demonstrating that what matters is the application. It would be pointless to attempt any Wellek-like extrapolation of the principles.

Comparing William Johnson Cory's much anthologized poem 'They told me Heraclitus' with Scott's 'Proud Maisie', Leavis shows that 'Heraclitus' 'seems to be all emotional comment, the alleged justifying situation, the subject of comment, being represented by loosely evocative generalities, about which the poet feels vaguely if "intensely" (the "intensity" of this kind of thing is conditioned by vagueness)'. In 'Proud Maisie' 'the emotion develops and defines itself as we grasp the dramatic elements the poem does offer – the data it presents (that is the effect) with emotional "disinterestedness".'

For Leavis in the forties, 'disinterestedness' was synomous with 'impersonality'. He also praises Wordsworth's 'A slumber did my spirit seal' by saying that something has been profoundly 'suffered as a personal calamity, but the experience has been so impersonalized that the effect, as much as that of 'Proud Maisie', is one of bare and disinterested presentment.' One disadvantage of reprinting a 1945 essay, barely revised, in a 1975 book is that we are given no means of judging how differently he would formulate his reactions to the poems today, now that he has recoiled so much further from T. S. Eliot's doctrine of impersonality. We again think of his discrimination between Eliot and Lawrence as critics when he uses the phrase 'spiritual health' in his attack on Tennyson's 'Break, break, break': 'The poet, we can say, whose habitual mode – whose emotional habit – was represented by that poem would not only be very limited; we should expect to find him noticeably given to certain weaknesses and vices.'

Comparing his 'Tears, idle tears' with Lawrence's 'Piano', Leavis finds banal phrases and swelling emotionality in both, but there is no counterpart in the Tennyson poem to Lawrence's success in focusing sharply on a specific scene, with a child 'sitting under the piano, in the boom of the tinkling strings'. 'The actuality of the remembered situation is unbeglamouring, becoming more so in the second stanza, with the "hymns" and the "tinkling piano". Something is, we see, held and presented in this poem, and the presenting involves an attitude towards, an element of disinterested valuation. For all the swell of emotion the critical mind has its part in the whole.' At the same time as being 'poignantly and inwardly conveyed', the 'flood of remembrance' is presented as if it were an 'object for contemplation'. Tennyson's poem 'moves simply forward with a sweetly plangent flow, without check, cross-tension or any qualifying element. To give it the reading it asks for is to flow with it, acquiescing in a complete and simple immersion.' Again one thinks, by contrast, of Coleridge's remarks on 'Venus and Adonis'.

Discussing Shelley, Leavis makes another allegation of 'spiritual malady'. His poetry offers feeling 'as something opposed to thought'. He is incapable of presenting 'any situation, any observed or imagined actuality, or any experience, as an object existing independently in its own nature and in its own right'. While Metaphysical conceits can be almost equally self-indulgent, when ingenuity is cultivated for its own sake, they are, at their best, 'obtrusive manifestations of an essential presence of "thought" such as we have in some non-Metaphysical poetry'. Though Marvell's 'Horatian Ode' is not one of his Metaphysical poems, the 'contemplating, relating and appraising mind is unmistakably there in the characteristic urbane poise . . . There could hardly have been a directer or more obviously disinterested concern with objects of contemplation: the attitudes seem to be wholly determined by the nature of what is seen and judged, and the expression of feeling to be secondary and merely incidental to just statement and presentment.'

In the essay on 'Imagery and Movement' Leavis exposes the fallacy of assuming that metaphor is 'essentially simile with the "like" or "as" left out'. Returning to the central point he had made in 1944 about Dr Johnson's limitations as a critic of Shakespeare,[1] Leavis argues that 'the English language in 1600 was an ideal medium for the Shakespearian processes of thought', but if Shakespeare had been 'born into Dryden's age, when Cartesian logic and "clarity" had triumphed', he would have been incapable of the 'quickness' that was 'essential for the apprehending and registering of subtleties and complexities'. The writer who subscribed to Augustan assumptions had cut himself off 'from most important capacities and potentialities of thought which of its nature is essentially heuristic and creative'. In saying that Shakespeare 'gives the image which he receives, not weakened or distorted by the intervention of any other mind', Johnson was reflecting the Lockean idea of perception as a passive

[1] This part of what was to have been a chapter on 'Imagery and Movement' was presumably written before the latter part which is printed in *Scrutiny* XIII 2, September 1945.

process of receiving impressions. But 'in major creative writers', language 'does unprecedented things, advances the frontiers of the known, and discovers the new.' Shakespeare's mind was not a receptacle: it went out to half-meet, half-create the images his language renders. His linguistic habit was incompatible with the stylistic discipline 'imposed by the great cultural change that had taken place, irreversibly, by the end of the seventeenth century. The "correctness" endorsed by Johnson amounted to the assumption that the map was the reality. It insisted that nothing mattered, or could be brought into intelligent discourse, that couldn't be rendered as explicit, clear, logical and grammatical statement.' Pedantic concern for the rules of syntax can be an obstacle in the way of construing a passage such as Antony's description of Octavia:

> Her tongue will not obey her heart, nor can
> Her heart inform her tongue – the swan's down-feather,
> That stands upon the swell at full of tide,
> And neither way inclines.

As Leavis says, there is no need to resolve the question of whether it is her heart or the inaction of heart and tongue that Shakespeare is comparing with the swan's down-feather: 'the relevant "meaning" – the communication in which the "image" plays its part – is created by the utterance as a totality, and is not a matter of separate local "meanings" put together more or less felicitously.'

In analysing complex verbal organization, 'it will not do to treat metaphors, images and other local effects as if their relation to the poem were at all like that of plums to cake.' The writer's tone and attitude are liable to be given less than their due if the analysis takes the form of paraphrase, and it is easy to forget that in a 'compressed simile', unlikeness can be as important as likeness. The example Leavis provides is Donne's line:

> Call countrey ants to harvest offices.

The metaphor derives its force as much from the dissimilarity as from the similarity between ants and farm-labourers, and it also suggests an attitude of good-humoured contempt. To the lovers in their curtained bedroom, the activities of ants and labourers are equally remote and irrelevant. 'It is from some such complexity as this, involving the telescoping or focal coincidence in the mind of contrasting or discrepant impressions or effects, that metaphor in general –

live metaphor – seems to derive its life: life involves friction and tension – a sense of arrest – in some degree.'

Looking at some excerpts from novels in the undated essay 'Prose', Leavis uses a passage which is probably by Captain Marryat as a foil to a very lively excerpt from Conrad's *A Personal Record*. The liveliness is shown to depend partly on specificity and freedom from cliché. 'Creative art here is an exercise in the achieving of precision (a process that is at the same time the achieving of complete sincerity – the elimination of ego-interested distortion and all impure motives) in the recovery of a memory now implicitly judged – implicitly, for actual judgment can't be stated – to be, in a specific life, of high significance. The evocation of concrete thisness begins in terms of the disciplined act of remembering, which, of course, is selective, and, in its re-creativity, creative, as all our achieved apprehension of the real must be.'

Conrad's phrase 'His white calves twinkled sturdily' is described by Leavis as 'a characteristically unprecedented collocation of words that we feel to have achieved itself instantaneously, with such inevitability does it make us see, and, in an implicitly evaluative way, realize and respond in a given total effect.' As he says, 'it is the creative writer who maintains the life and potentiality of the language.'

'The value of a review must be judged by its attitude to the living literature of the time.' This principle of *The Calendar*'s had been quoted by Leavis in his Introduction to *Towards Standards of Criticism*, and if it is true of a review it must also be true of a critic and teacher, though Leavis was damaged less seriously, less noticeably and more gradually than *Scrutiny* was by his failure to keep in touch. Perhaps *The Great Tradition* would have been even better if it had been conceived in terms of a complementary relationship with another book by Leavis called *New Bearings in English Fiction*, but it does have a complementary relationship with *D. H. Lawrence: Novelist*.

Alongside his writing and his editorial work, Leavis went on doing excellent work as a teacher, attracting good students to Downing, helping them to think for themselves, helping them to achieve good results in the examinations, and helping them in other less obvious ways. In November 1950 Geoffrey Strickland and Morris Shapira asked Leavis whether they could use his room for a meeting about the Korean War. General MacArthur had not yet been sacked, napalm was being used and an eye-witness report was to be delivered by a lady doctor who was also a Labour councillor. But the meeting was liable to be disrupted by the rugger-playing college 'hearties' who had already broken up Strickland's and Shapira's rooms since they had formed their protest group. Yes, said Leavis, he knew the kind of person they were up against, and he could attend the meeting himself. 'I can be very useful in a rough house.' Probably it would be wiser if he didn't come, but certainly they could use his room. They should be careful, though, not to let the communists take advantage of them. At anti-fascist meetings in the thirties, he had found himself sitting on a platform covered with hammers and sickles, despite assurances that it was a 'non-party' protest.

He had retained his athletic prowess, keeping fit and running home every night. During one bout of post-war insomnia, when his doctor suggested he should run himself to sleep, he started a routine of long-distance running. He prided himself on his swimming, his rope-climbing and his skating. When the river froze, he would skate to

Grantchester. And sometimes he would read his students Swinburne's
Chorus from *Atalanta*, 'When the hounds of spring are on winter's
traces . . .' only to stop in the middle. 'I'm sorry, gentlemen. I can
swim fifty yards under water, but I can't read this!'

In 1953, six years after his wife had stopped working for it, Leavis
decided he could not keep *Scrutiny* alive. The final issue, the 76th,
was dated October.

> But this is the moment for the parting salute; a sad moment, many
> times postponed, but now an inevitable one. We have carried on,
> without secretary, without business-manager, without publicity
> manager, and without publicity, for two full decades.

As he wrote in his dignified 'Valedictory', once the war had dispersed
his nucleus of collaborators it had been impossible to recreate it.
With fewer writers who could be commissioned to produce work of a
high enough standard and more who let him down after making firm
promises, he had often been forced to serialize work that contributors
were doing anyway. Writing his letters by hand, courteously and
meticulously, he had found it hard to keep up with the unavoidable
correspondence. More important, it was becoming increasingly difficult to publish punctually. But even if *Scrutiny* had sunk somewhat
below its pre-war standard, the Leavises deserved very much more
acknowledgment than they received for keeping it going so long. As
soon as its demise was announced, letters of protest and condolence
poured through their letter-box. But, as he wrote in his 1962 Retrospect, 'no one who could be thought of as a voice of the "English"
Establishment – at Cambridge, or in the country – was heard from
on this occasion. And *The Times* refused to print a letter of testimony
to the work of *Scrutiny* from Professor Henri Fluchère, Director of the
Maison Française at Oxford. The distinguished military figure at the
head of the British Council, however, sent us a few proper lines of
official condolence, hoping we should believe that the Council had
always done its best for *Scrutiny*, and ending: "I hope you will soon
start another magazine."'

His own last contribution to *Scrutiny*, an essay on Lawrence's story
'The Captain's Doll', had been incomplete. 'To be concluded' said
the italicized note after his signature, and it was concluded in
D. H. Lawrence: Novelist, which came out in 1955, the sixth and last
of his books to depend almost entirely on material that had appeared
in *Scrutiny*. Again the editor was inefficient and left in a sentence

which said Lawrence had been writing *Women in Love* 'thirty years ago'.

The pattern of Leavis's writing, like the pattern of his life, had to change. His teaching continued, he made occasional contributions to American critical anthologies and literary reviews, wrote occasional book reviews and letters to the press, but no longer having a reliable outlet for his essays, he produced fewer. He had been working inordinately hard for very little money and scarcely taking any holidays abroad. In the early fifties he made one of his few visits to France – at the invitation of an American research student who had a house there. In 1954, at the age of fifty-nine, he was finally invited on to the Board of the English Faculty, thanks to A. P. Rossiter, a lecturer who rallied his colleagues with his insistence that the invitation was absurdly overdue. But it was not until five years later that Leavis was appointed University Reader in English, a position he then held for only three years.

11 D. H. Lawrence

'He stands where one can't get at him. And he burns with life. And where does his life come from, to him? That's the mystery. That great burning life in him, that never is dead. Most men have a deadness in them, that frightens me so because of my own deadness. Why can't men get their life straight, like St Mawr, and then think? Why can't they think quick, mother: quick as a woman: only farther than we do? Why isn't men's thinking quick like fire, mother? Why is it so slow, so dead, so deadly dull?'

One answer to Lou de Witt's question could be given in terms of the developments in industrialism, in social organization and in the language, which make it impossible to think today in the way that Shakespeare thought. We may try to sidestep the clichés that are propagated by television, newspapers, advertisements and pop culture, but it is impossible to be unaware of them and impossible to create new phrases in such profusion as the best Elizabethan writers did, by letting the mind go out to greet a new experience and grouping words energetically together so that the reader or listener can savour the energy in the action imitated. Reviewing an anthology of Elizabethan prose,[1] L. C. Knights said the 'muscular content' of the language was then 'an important part of its "meaning", and it was this, together with the reading habits fostered by speaking such a language, that enabled physical states to be portrayed with such immediacy'.

Like Knights, Leavis was deeply influenced by Eliot's theory that there had been a 'dissociation of sensibility' in the seventeenth century. Eliot had borrowed the phrase from Rémy de Gourmont, who was unlike Eliot in believing that in a great writer life and work were inseparable. 'Sensibility' meant 'le pouvoir général de sentir' and it included the faculty of reason, 'qui n'est que de la sensibilité cristallisée'. In his 1921 essay on 'The Metaphysical Poets' Eliot tried to analyse

something which had happened to the mind of England between the time of Donne or Lord Herbert of Cherbury and the time of Tennyson

[1] In *Scrutiny* II 4, March 1934.

and Browning; it is the difference between the intellectual poet and the reflective poet. .... The poets of the seventeenth century, the successors of the dramatists of the sixteenth, possessed a mechanism of sensibility which could devour any kind of experience. They are simple, artificial, difficult, or fantastic, as their predecessors were; no less nor more than Dante, Guido Cavalcanti, Guinicelli, or Cino. In the seventeenth century a dissociation of sensibility set in, from which we have never recovered; and this dissociation, as is natural, was aggravated by the influence of the two most powerful poets of the century, Milton and Dryden.

Twenty-six years later, in his British Academy lecture on Milton, Eliot back-pedalled into some qualifications:

> To lay the burden on the shoulders of Milton and Dryden was a mistake. If such a dissociation did take place, I suspect that the causes are too complex and too profound to justify our accounting for the change in terms of literary criticism. All we can say is, that something like this did happen; that it had something to do with the Civil War; that it would even be unwise to say it was caused by the Civil War, but that it is a consequence of the same causes which brought about the Civil War; that we must seek the causes in Europe, not in England alone; and for what these causes were, we may dig and dig until we get to a depth at which words and concepts fail us.

It is true that, as with the idea of an 'organic community', one can step back further and further into history, uncovering evidence that the disintegration had already begun. Frank Kermode[1] shows that there is a relationship between the 'undissociated' sensibility and religious faith in the unity of all experience, internal and external. He argues that 'if we were to pursue the dissociation back into the past, we should find ourselves in Athens. Elizabethan "atheism" was far more than a scientific issue; there was genuine anxiety, a real "naturalist" movement widely affecting ethical and political conduct ... we shall never find a state of culture worth bothering about (from the literary point of view, that is) in which language is so primitive as to admit no thinking that is not numinous; in which there is no possibility of a naturalist assault on the society's beliefs.' He goes on to suggest: 'The theory of the dissociation of sensibility is, in fact, the most successful version of a Symbolist attempt to explain why the modern world resists works of art that testify to the poet's special,

[1] In his valuable chapter on 'Dissociation of Sensibility' in *Romantic Image*. Routledge 1957.

anti-intellectual way of knowing truth. . . . The historical effort of
Symbolism has been to identify a period happily ignorant of the war
between Image and discourse, an undissociated age.'

   This was why T. E. Hulme reacted so strongly when Ezra Pound
spoke to him about the difference between Cavalcanti's 'precise
interpretative metaphor, and the Petrarchian fustian and ornament'.
Cavalcanti, a contemporary of Dante, produced integrated images,
phrases that corresponded accurately to the original sensation,
whereas Petrarch, the herald of the Renaissance, was 'a poet of the
ornamental image, the image appended to discourse, the flower stuck
in sand'. Rémy de Gourmont's suggestion that symbolism in poetry
corresponded to idealism in philosophy throws an interesting side-
light on Kermode's point about Eliot's theory.

   Bloomsbury culture took over the symbolist idea of non-referential
art. Clive Bell defined visual art as 'Significant Form', maintaining
that 'Pure Art Value' or pure aesthetic experience cannot be judged
in relationship to the experience of ordinary living. Lawrence hated
the idea that art could be insulated from life. He introduces the
subject explicitly at a crucial point in the development of *Women in
Love*, when Gudrun is siding with the wizened little Loerke, who is
arguing that his sculpture of a small naked girl on a horse

> has no relation with the everyday world of this and other, there is no
> connection between them, absolutely none, they are two different and
> distinct planes of existence, and to translate one into the other is worse
> than foolish, it is a darkening of all counsel, a making confusion every-
> where. Do you see, you *must not* confuse the relative work of action, with
> the absolute world of art.

Ursula becomes very angry with them:

> The world of art is only the truth about the real world, that's all – but
> you are too far gone to see it.

The development of the sequence discredits Loerke when it reveals
that he takes a perverted interest in the young art students he uses as
models. 'I don't like them any bigger, any older. Then they are
beautiful, at sixteen, seventeen, eighteen – after that, they are no use
to me.'

   Leavis neither attacked nor defended the 'dissociation of sensibility' theory until 1967, when, in his Clark Lectures, he praised 'the
essential and pregnant felicity of the critical constatation that Eliot

focuses in the phrase'. In 1969, he discussed it in more detail.[1] Eliot's insight, he said, was incontestable: 'for does anyone question that in the seventeenth century a momentous total change in civilization took place, so that by its close we have the modern world, launched on its accelerating advance towards the consummation we now know?' The change was 'manifested in the English language' and most notably in its 'literary use'. Dryden's treatment of *Antony and Cleopatra* provided a disturbing indication of what had occurred. In describing the Metaphysical poets as 'successors of the dramatists', Eliot revealed a curious reluctance to name Shakespeare's plays as the crucible in which the vernacular was pressurized into sophisticated art. What Eliot learned from Donne, Donne learned from Shakespeare. Eliot's 'effects, achieved with masterly precision, depend upon his appealing to the reader's sense of how things go naturally in the living spoken language and the speaking voice. Thus he exercises, in the only way possible, a subtle command of shifting tone, inflexion, distance and tempo.' Augustanism involved a separation between 'polite' and 'popular', which was well advanced by the end of the eighteenth century, 'working inevitable destruction upon the inherited civilization of the people. Dickens was the last great writer to enjoy something of the Shakespearean advantage.' Leavis argues[2] that it is the great novelists who are

> the successors of Shakespeare; for in the nineteenth century and later the strength – the poetic and creative strength – of the English language goes into prose fiction. In comparison the formal poetry is a marginal affair. And the achievement of T. S. Eliot, remarkable as it was, did not reverse the relation.

Lawrence is 'our last great writer; he is still the great writer of our own phase of civilization . . . Yet, though he was supremely intelligent, with the intelligence that manifests itself in a rare degree of self-knowledge, clearly his peculiar experience of emotional forcing, strain and painful readjustment had some lasting consequences that made it very difficult for him to be sure of his poise and centrality as a reporter on some of the most delicate problems his genius drove him to explore.' He also had to contend with the anaemia in the language. The best of his prose is richly textured and poetic, but no-one could

[1] 'English, Unrest and Continuity'. A lecture at Gregynog for the University of Wales. The text is reprinted in *Nor Shall My Sword*.
[2] *D. H. Lawrence: Novelist*.

have taken so many creative risks without lapsing sometimes into jargon, stridency, over-explicitness and repetitiousness. Just as the repetition of a single word is sometimes indispensable to the rhythmic effect he needs, over-insistence is the result of lacking a poise he could not have been expected to achieve. It was impossible for him to avoid placing too much weight on such words as 'burning', 'life', 'blood', 'terror', 'throb', 'annihilate'. That he was aware of this weakness is proved by the self-parody he puts into the letter of Birkin's which is read out in Chapter 28 of *Women in Love*, 'Gudrun in the Pompadour'.

But his lapses have received too much attention and his achievements too little. It is remarkable that he succeeded as well as he did in using the language creatively and heuristically. As Leavis says, his genius drove him to explore the most delicate problems. 'To have found, as he contemplated human life, or lives, in the contemporary world, the answers he was looking for, Lawrence would have had to be more than a great creative writer – he would have had to be something hardly conceivable.' But his fiction reports truthfully on his investigation, and he was a great writer in Rémy de Gourmont's sense: life and work were inseparable. Leavis argues that the imperfection of *The Rainbow* as a work of art is 'an aspect of the unique positive value, the achieved significance, of what has been done. For *The Rainbow* exemplifies in a special way the peculiar Laurentian genius: the extraordinary power of the impersonalizing intelligence to maintain, while the artist, in an intensely personal exploratory way, is actually living the experience that goes into the art, the conditions that make creative impersonality possible. When Lawrence started *The Rainbow* he knew that it was only by further living – not by mere further pondering of experience already lived – that he could complete it.'

Leavis's commentary on *The Rainbow* is extremely fine. Lawrence's attitude to life, unlike Flaubert's or T. S. Eliot's, is radically positive. The manner is reverent without idealization, tender without sentimentality. The novel belongs to the same tradition of art as George Eliot's fiction, making an important contribution to social history. It 'shows us the transmission of the spiritual heritage in an actual society, and shows it in relation to the general development of civilization'. Lawrence also belongs to the same ethical and religious tradition as George Eliot. An interest like his 'in the deeper life of the psyche cannot be an interest in the individual abstracted from the society to which he belongs'. He believed that he was penetrating 'really a stratum deeper than I think anybody has ever gone in a novel', and he starts his story in the 1840s, when 'the immemorial farm-life ("We've been here above two hundred years") and the England represented by the canal, the colliery, the colliery-town and the advancing railway met one another and consorted in a challenging paradigm'. By ranging over three generations, the narrative can illustrate what it was like to be brought up in the environment of a living tradition. 'We are made to see how, amid the pieties and continuities of life at the Marsh, the spiritual achievements of a mature civilization – the integrative sanctions, with the value-creating associations and forms that make possible the individual's attainment, above the level of mere response to basic instinct, of something rich and significant – are transmitted.' We see the old religious habits, the perennial craving for spiritual fulfilment speaking through the individual, who is never pushed so far into the foreground as he is in *Women in Love*.

Writing about E. M. Forster,[1] Lawrence complained that he ignored the undercurrents of life, seeing 'people, people and nothing but people *ad nauseam*'. Lawrence puts his characters into a context formed partly by the religious tradition which has conditioned their attitudes and needs, and he makes them unsatisfied with each other when they seem self-contained in their individuality. What Ursula cannot bear about Skrebensky is that 'She knew him all round, not on any side did he lead into the unknown. Poignant, almost passionate appreciation she felt for him but none of the rich fear, the connexion with the unknown, or the reverence of love.' And like Hardy's characters – but more convincingly – Lawrence's are rooted into the natural environment. When Tom Brangwen is outside in 'the darkest of twilight' looking through the kitchen window at the Polish woman who will be his wife, he is being propelled towards the moment of action by forces that are not independent of the bare trees that drum and whistle in the booming wind or 'the clouds which packed in great, alarming haste across the dark sky'. Leavis's commentary focuses on the unimportance of decision and willpower. '"He did not think of anything, only knew that the wind was blowing." What we have here, of course, is not relaxedness or distraction; he perceives "out of the depths of his stillness", where the whole resolution is gathered – the stillness being set off by the outer stresses and disturbances. The needs and profound purposes that it unites are there in

[1] *Letters to Martin Secker*

the intensity of the perceptions in which they register themselves, undistracted by his "thinking of anything"; the intensity, on examination, we recognize to be a matter of their charge of significance.'

Lawrence is unlike George Eliot in his 'intense apprehension of the unity of life'. The novel cannot but be frustrating to readers with an insatiable appetite for character and the kind of climax that comes as a culmination after protracted suspense, but the apprehension of unity is beautifully served by 'the complex rhythm organizing the book – the movement that, by recurrence along with newness, brings continually a significant recall of what has gone before'. But it is a novel which needs to be read with extreme care, and the frequency of misunderstandings proves the need for some such commentary as Leavis's. Lawrence is still liable to be dismissed as a prophet of the Dark Gods, and his references to 'blood intimacy' and 'blood-togetherness' are still being confused with Nazi propaganda about *Blut und Boden*, although Leavis has pointed out that in *The Rainbow* the life of 'blood-intimacy' is 'a necessary and potent presence as something to be transcended. The novel has for theme the urgency, and the difficult struggle, of the higher human possibilities to realize themselves.'

It is strange that Leavis should go on to make the mistake of drawing an equation between Tom Brangwen and 'the full, complex human psyche, with all its potentialities'. Surely H. M. Daleski is right to suggest[1] that 'we are intended to regard him as essentially a creature of the dark, as a man who aspires towards the light – who aspires, that is to say, to realize his "man-being" – but who cannot, unaided, incorporate the light in a unified self'. Leavis seems to be aware of Tom's incompleteness when he quotes Lawrence's reference to 'the disillusion of his first carnal contact with woman, strengthened by his innate desire to find in a woman the embodiment of all his inarticulate, powerful religious impulses'. But Daleski gives us a clearer impression than Leavis does of the significance of the novel's structure: the realization of full human potential is 'seen to be dependent on effective "utterance" in the "man's world", and Tom and Will and Skrebensky', the male representatives of the three generations, are 'in different measure, condemned for a failure in manhood'. It is only Ursula who can 'be said to have achieved full individuality'. Ursula is the most Lawrence-like character in the

[1] In *The Forked Flame: A Study of D. H. Lawrence*. Faber 1965.

book. He has ascribed to her many of his own beliefs, many of his own experiences, remodelled for the change of gender. This is one reason for the discontinuity with the Ursula of *Women in Love*, who is less Lawrence-like because Rupert Birkin is there as his representative.

In 1921[1] Lawrence said 'I like *Women in Love* best of all my books'. But in 1916, when it was not quite finished, he had written to Catherine Carswell[2]: 'The book frightens me: it is so end-of-the-world. But it is, it must be, the beginning of a new world too.' The emphasis, though, was on making an end. Describing it, the following July, in a letter to Waldo Frank, he said: 'This actually does contain the results in one's soul of the war: it is purely destructive, not like *The Rainbow*, destructive – consummating.' In February 1916 Lawrence wrote to Ottoline Morell: 'This world of ours has got to collapse now, in violence and injustice and destruction, nothing will stop it. . . . The only thing now to be done is either to go down with the ship, sink with the ship, or, as much as one can, leave the ship, and like a castaway live a life apart. As for me, I do not belong to the ship; I will not, if I can help it, sink with it. I will not live any more in this time. I know what it is. I reject it. As far as I possibly can, I will stand outside this time, I will live my life, and, if possible, be happy, though the whole world slides in horror down into the bottomless pit.' Daleski interprets the novel in terms of this letter:

> Both couples are shown to be on board a ship which is rapidly heading for destruction, and their personal relations are not only qualified by their response to the danger but are the measure of a psychic drive towards life or death which such a predicament intensifies.

Leavis considers the achievement of *The Rainbow* to be surpassed by that of *Women in Love*, which he calls 'one of the most striking works of creative originality that fiction has to show'. But his commentary does not plumb the depths of the novel's nihilism, and it does not sufficiently qualify what has been said in 'Lawrence and Class' – a chapter placed earlier in the book (though written later) – about the positiveness of Lawrence's radical attitude to life, his 'reverence' and his 'tenderness'. These are qualities which appear strikingly in *The Rainbow*, but there are no counterparts in *Women in Love* to the

---

[1] Letter to Douglas Goldring, 4 April.
[2] 7 November.

superbly unsentimental scene in which Tom takes his unhappy little stepdaughter out to watch him feeding the cows or the sequence in which the young Ursula helps her father to plant potatoes.

Women in Love is more tightly organized than *The Rainbow*. As Leavis says, there is 'not a scene, episode, image or touch but forwards the organized development of the themes'. He is also right to dismiss the idea 'that an abstract system of schematic simplifications has been imposed on life'. Lawrence's 'discursive thought itself is governed by a distrust of abstractions that, positively, is a rare power of maintaining a living fidelity to the concrete; and the mind that has done this thinking brings to the artist's creative work a sharpened perception of the significance and a strengthened grasp of it'. But Mark Kinkead-Weeks[1] has pointed shrewdly to what differentiates *Women in Love* from *The Rainbow*: Lawrence had learnt 'to hold the apocalyptic in that odd tension with the colloquial'. The main statement of *The Rainbow* is about tradition and evolution, and it has to be made through the narrative and the drama because the characters are themselves incapable of analysing the currents in the tide of developing consciousness that is carrying them forward; the main statement of *Women in Love* is about the plight of civilization. The characters are incomparably more articulate, and too much of what Lawrence has to say is put straight into their mouths. The lapses into jargon are comparatively rare but the prose is less poetic, less original, less exploratory and thinner-textured than it was in the earlier novel. Leavis does not pay enough attention either to the language – in which images of decay are recurrent – or to the apocalyptic element.

The best brief account of the novel is given by Frank Kermode in *Lawrence*.[2] 'It is not a novel of extended arcs, like its predecessor; it proceeds by awful discontinuous leaps; its progress enacts those desperate religious plunges into an unknown Lawrence so much wanted.' The individual spirit, the race and the world are already at the end of their tether when the story begins, like *Middlemarch*, with two girls talking about marriage. 'They walk into the colliery landscape, chthonic, post-mortem, a landscape of ghouls, hideous but with a strange inhuman vitality. The machine has turned England and its people into this kind of underworld: the English have led the rush into dissolution. Before the first chapter is over we have seen

[1] 'The Marble and the Statue' in *Imagined Worlds*, eds. Maynard Mack and Ian Gregor, 1968.
[2] Fontana 1973.

Gudrun choose Gerald, master of the ghouls, his icy beauty representing a Nordic depth of corruption; and we have seen Hermione as an image of the passional life corruptly led in the mind.' At Hermione's house, Breadalby, the conversation is 'like a rattle of small artillery'.

Leavis cites a passage from Lawrence's *Psychoanalysis and the Unconscious* which illuminates Gerald's decline:

> So we see the brain, like a great dynamo and accumulator, accumulating mechanical force and presuming to apply this mechanical force-control to the living unconscious, subjecting everything spontaneous to certain machine-principles called ideals or ideas.

Gerald is like Loerke, the sculptor: 'both artist and industrialist accept, from their different points of view, the triumph of mechanism and the implicit reduction of human life to mere instrumentality.' Leavis is good on Hermione's unsuccessful use of willpower to conquer her own inadequacy. His analysis of the 'see-saw battle' between Gerald and Gudrun is useful, but too brief. And Daleski is right to challenge Leavis's assertion that Lawrence makes a 'sufficiently clear . . . sufficiently cogent' statement of the norm that Birkin proposes for the male-female relationship. 'I think that Lawrence's attempt to portray Birkin and Ursula's achievement of "the pure duality of polarization" (with all that the phrase, in its context, implies) is as unsatisfactory and unconvincing as the "doctrinal" passages in which he makes a frontal attack on our credence, and as the "symbolic" scenes in which he presents external support for his position.'

Leavis is certainly right to concentrate on *The Rainbow* and *Women in Love* as Lawrence's best novels, and he has performed a valuable function in boosting their popularity at the expense of the too directly autobiographical *Sons and Lovers*. But his preference for *Women in Love* does not seem to accord with the criteria that have previously been most important to him. Plot and language are less heuristic; statement is more explicit and less dramatic; the attitude to life is more negative; and altogether the novel is less in line with the Great Tradition.

Leavis's books were selling extremely well. By 1962 *Culture and Environment* had been reprinted seven times and *Revaluation* four times. *New Bearings* and *Education and the University*, which had both come out in new editions, were in their fourth and second impressions. *D. H. Lawrence: Novelist* was already in its third, and when Penguin Books brought out *The Common Pursuit* as a Peregrine at 7/6, it sold 10,000 copies within six weeks. *The Great Tradition*, which had been reprinted twice in hardback, was also published as a Peregrine in 1962. *Revaluation* and *D. H. Lawrence: Novelist* both came out as Peregrines in 1964, but without *Scrutiny* as an interim publication base, Leavis had little incentive to put a new book together. Twelve years were to elapse before *D. H. Lawrence: Novelist* was followed by *Anna Karenina and Other Essays*.

At the same time as paperbacks were widening his public, his attack on C. P. Snow brought him more publicity than he had ever had. During the mid-fifties, as a book-reviewer in *The Sunday Times*, Snow had spoken out in favour of him, but it was now essential to counteract the damage Snow was inflicting as the printed version of his 1959 Rede lecture on *The Two Cultures and the Scientific Revolution* was filtering into schools. From the scholarship papers he marked, Leavis had realized that 'sixth-form masters were making their bright boys read Snow as doctrinal, definitive and formative – and a good examination investment'.

The Two Cultures was already in its sixth impression when Leavis bought a copy. A polite criticism of Snow might have had little effect. Leavis had once said of D. W. Harding that he didn't understand the value of aggression: he himself did understand, and he never made better use of his understanding than on 28 February 1962 in the Hall of Downing College, when he delivered his Richmond lecture on *Two Cultures? The Significance of C.P. Snow*. The beginning is reminiscent of Auden's deflation of Churchill:

Anyone who offers to speak with inwardness and authority on both science and literature will be conscious of more than ordinary powers,

but one can imagine such consciousness going with a certain modesty –
with a strong sense, indeed, of a limited range and a limited warrant. The
peculiar quality of Snow's assurance expresses itself in a pervasive tone;
a tone of which one can say that, while only genius could justify it, one
cannot readily think of genius adopting it.

As an example of Snow's tone Leavis quoted:

> The only writer of world-class who seems to have had an understanding
> of the industrial revolution was Ibsen in his old age: and there wasn't
> much that old man didn't understand.

To demonstrate that Snow's way of handling words was extremely
loose, Leavis picked on his claims that scientists 'have the future in
their bones' while the representatives of 'the traditional culture' are
'natural Luddites'.

Leavis also discussed the gap between Snow's reputation and his
achievement as a novelist. This was relevant to Leavis's attack on the
materialism implicit in Snow's characteristically phrased declaration
that 'common men can show astonishing fortitude in chasing jam
tomorrow. Jam today, and men aren't at their noblest. The trans-
formations have also provided something which only the scientific
culture can take in its stride. Yet, when we don't take it in our
stride, it makes us look silly.' Snow did almost nothing to substantiate
his assumption that a separate culture had been generated out of
scientists' technical knowledge and their specialized methods of
enquiry. He was, as Leavis points out, merely abusing the word
'culture'. And as Michael Yudkin, a bio-chemist, argued in a
critique of Snow which has been printed alongside Leavis's lecture[1],
'There are, regrettably, dozens of cultures in Sir Charles's use of the
term, even if the gap between the scientist and the non-scientist is
probably the widest. . . . There will be no building of a bridge across
the gap, no appearance of modern Leonardos, no migration of scientists to literature. Instead there will be the atrophy of the traditional
culture, and its gradual annexation by the scientific – annexation
not of territory but of men. It may not be long before only a single
culture remains.'

Although no journalists had been admitted to the lecture, garbled
reports of it began to appear in the press, and it would be far better,
Leavis decided, to have it printed verbatim. Still having no secre-

[1] In *Two Cultures: The Significance of C. P. Snow.*

tary, he had never had it typed out, and when *The Spectator* published it in the issue dated 9 March, the printer had to work from Leavis's handwriting. The text was illustrated with four cartoons of Snow and one of Leavis.

He must have expected a controversy to develop, but he must have been surprised by the quantity of animosity he had aroused. There were so many indignant letters to the Editor of *The Spectator* that only a small proportion could be printed, even by devoting five pages to them. William Gerhardi took six and a half columns to accuse Leavis of trying 'to assassinate the reputation of an eminent contemporary'. Dame Edith Sitwell denounced the lecture as 'a silly exhibition'. She had read to the end 'with an entire lack of interest, but some surprise'. (Later she said: 'Dr Leavis only attacked Charles because he is famous and writes good English'). G. S. Fraser called Leavis's critical regime 'a Robespierrian one, of Virtue and Terror'. He also compared Leavis with Cicero, praising the lecture as 'one of the greatest rhetorical performances I have ever read'. Not one letter came out unequivocally on Leavis's side until the following week, when the correspondence occupied over seven columns, ending with a letter from Bernard Miles offering Snow 'the hospitality of the Mermaid Theatre on any Sunday evening during the next six months'.

On 30 March two-and-a-half columns of the editorial were devoted to 'The Two Cultures': 'It is hard not to agree with Dr Leavis when he criticizes Sir Charles's view of culture', and there were three columns of letters. The correspondence ended on 6 April with a letter from a lecturer at the University of Nairobi: 'There are of course no two cultures, except in a *Reader's Digest* sense.'

Meanwhile the controversy had spread into other papers. *The Times Literary Supplement* devoted a leading article to it on 23 March and correspondence ensued. That Leavis did not succeed in killing the fallacy of cultural dualism is evidenced by Lord Robbins's book *The University and the Modern World* and by the incorporation of Robbins's ideas into the Labour Party's educational policy. So it would be harder today than it was in 1962 to argue that the ammunition Leavis used was too heavy for his purpose.

Snow's prophecy of a future dominated by scientists must have reminded Leavis of Gerald Crich and Lawrence's warnings about the dangers of reducing human life to mere instrumentality. 'It's the loss of ends and significance in the complication of the machinery: all ends having authority lost, all but those lending themselves to statistical mensuration – as reductive "equality" does.'[1]

Lawrence had ridiculed egalitarianism. As Birkin says to Hermione, 'We are all different and unequal in spirit – it is only the social differences that are based on accidental material conditions. We are all abstractly or mathematically equal, if you like . . . But I, myself, who am myself, what have I to do with equality with any other man or woman? In the spirit, I am as separate as one star is from another, as different in quality and quantity. Establish a state on that.' To Leavis it is obvious that 'The problem is to re-establish an effective educated public, for it is only in the existence of an educated public, capable of responding and making its response felt, that "standards" can be there for the critic to appeal to'. And, as he added the following year[2], 'the more you extend higher education – and especially in an age of technological aids and Open Universities . . . the more insidious becomes the menace to standards and more potent and unashamed the animus against them. Unless standards are maintained somewhere the whole community is let down, and higher education itself is not exempt from the consequences. The only place where standards can be maintained is the university properly conceived – the university as Lord Robbins, Lord Annan, Mr Fowler, Minister of State overseeing higher education, and Mr Harold Wilson are committed to destroying it.'

In his 1967 Clark lectures at Cambridge he had redefined his idea of the university: 'The real university is a centre of consciousness and human responsibility for the civilized world; it is a creative centre of civilization,' which must maintain 'the living heritage on which meaning and humane intelligence depend.' Matthew Arnold had understood that to preserve a continuity of culture consciousness, intelligence needed to be used more deliberately than ever before. 'It was the main concern of his life to promote in this country the steps and the process that should create (this being their ideal aim) a class of the educated – a class that could be definable and thought of as essentially and unequivocally that, in dissociation from the idea of social privilege.' But today there is an endemic rage – especially among intellectuals – against the idea of an intellectual élite.

In 1963 or 4, when Richard Crossman was Shadow Minister for

[1] '"English", Unrest and Continuity'.
[2] '"Literarism" versus "Scientism"', a 1970 lecture at Bristol, printed in *Nor Shall My Sword*.

Education, he asked a friend to introduce him to Leavis, who later described the meeting in *Nor Shall My Sword*:

> He began by raising an issue that involved the difficult and delicate problem of getting anything done towards the achieving of the real university, and raised it in such a way as to make it plain that the problem didn't exist for him. Faced with nothing I could offer to discuss, I merely said 'What are you going to do about it when you're a government?' He paused for a moment; then, lifting a rhetorical fist, replied with impressive resolution as one disposing of the essential problem: 'We'll smash the oligarchy.' Reminded in this discouraging way of the truth that politicians, with inevitable consequences for their habits of thought, necessarily think first of winning the next election, I could only return, 'There are oligarchies everywhere', adding that there were even said to be oligarchies in *his* democratic party . . . I knew he belonged to a powerful one, and aspired to belong to a powerfuller. Human nature manifests itself very commonly in that way.

Leavis is not a Conservative. The only political party he has ever supported is the Liberal Party, and, as he says, he is 'not more opposed to democracy than Lord Annan or Mr Harold Wilson himself is'. In the late sixties, when there was a local by-election, he subscribed to the Liberal candidate's fund. Addressing a public meeting, Jeremy Thorpe said that the Liberal Party stood for comprehensive schools. The candidate seemed less like an educated man than the previous Liberal candidate for Cambridge, and even he had been careful to reassure the constituency that there was no danger of his showing any undemocratic bias if the interests of the city were in conflict with those of the university. 'And I have been forced,' wrote Leavis, 'to abandon the illusion that I could show my sense of political responsibility by believing, or trying to believe, in any party.'[1]

The withdrawal from party politics was not accompanied by any withdrawal from social commitment. Leavis's preoccupations had never been 'merely literary': 'I don't believe in any "literary values" . . . the judgments the literary critic is concerned with are judgments about life.' But the Clark Lectures and *Nor Shall My Sword* are less concerned with literary criticism than his previous books. The main preoccupation is 'to find a way to save cultural continuity, that continuous collaborative renewal which keeps the "heritage" of perception, judgment, responsibility and spiritual awareness alive, responsive to change, and authoritative for guidance'. Leavis's writing

[1] *English Literature in Our Time.*

in his cultural criticism is less concentrated, more repetitious and more anecdotal than usual, but one of the reasons it is valuable is that he engages so directly with the question of why the cultural heritage is worth preserving. What is the relevance of the great tradition to the problems of a rapidly changing society?

One answer is that 'In coming to terms with great literature we discover what at bottom we really believe. What for – what ultimately for? What do men live by? – the questions work and tell at what I can only call a religious depth of thought and feeling.' His use of the word 'religious', like his use of the word 'spiritual', cannot but be slightly disturbing to the anti-transcendentalist. But as he says,[1] 'My own recourse to the word "spiritual" (and all imporant words are dangerous) is determined by the contemplation of a world in which the technologico-Benthamite ethos has triumphed at the expense of human spirit – that is, of human life.' There are grave dangers of a disastrous outcome to the current cultural crisis, and Leavis has realized how urgent the need is 'to get essential recognition' for the fact 'that major creative writers are concerned with a necessary kind of thought'. If literature is not considered as 'thought' or as 'necessary', it will not be rated highly by the educational legislators.

In 'Thought, Language and Objectivity', the first chapter in *The Living Principle*, Leavis makes out an excellent case for the defence. 'In major literary works,' he argues, 'we have the fullest use of language,' which involves 'creative imprecision . . . The discipline that maintains the standards of science has its existence in a specializing community, the intellectual devotion of which is a special and professional morality.' But the dry precision of the scientific language depends on the life of the language used by the community. Leavis quotes from Marjorie Grene's *The Knower and the Known*:[2]

Mother and child, as Buytendijk says, already form a society. The child's discovery, and construction, of the world already takes place with and through others, through question and answer, through social play, through the older child's or the adult's interpretation of pictures, the teaching of language and writing – all the way to the research student's training in the school of a master. All the way we are shaping ourselves on the model of or in criticism of others, and of the standards

[1] 'Eliot's Classical Standing' in *Lectures in America*.
[2] Faber 1966.

embodied in the lives of others. . . . No discipline, however 'factual', however 'detached', can come into being or remain in existence except in so far as the fundamental evaluative acts of the individuals belonging to a given culture have legislated into existence and maintain in existence the area of free inquiry and of mutual confirmation or falsification which such inquiry demands.

Without language, then, there could have been no human world, and Leavis has understood how the creativity of the artist is 'continuous with the general human creativity that, having created the human world we live in, keeps it renewed and real . . . The nature of livingness in human life is manifest in language – manifest to those whose thought about language *is*, inseparably, thought about literary creation. They can't but realize more than notionally that a language is more than a means of expression; it is the heuristic conquest won out of representative experience, the upshot or precipitate of immemorial human living, and embodies values, distinctions, identifications, conclusions, promptings, cartographical hints and tested potentialities. It exemplifies the truth that life is growth and growth change, and the condition of these is continuity.'

The chapter deals rather summarily with Wittgenstein and the critics who apply linguistic analysis to literature, but he makes a good point when he insists: 'Thought about language should entail the full and firm recognition that words "mean" because individual human beings have meant the meaning, and that there is no meaning unless individual beings can meet in it, the completing of the element of "intend" being represented by the responding someone's certitude that the last condition obtains. Individual human beings can meet in a meaning because language – or let us rather say a language, meaning the English language (for there is no such thing as language in general) – is for them in any present a living actuality that is organically one with the "human world" they, in growing up into it, have naturally taken for granted. There is in the language a central core in which for generations individual speakers have met.' The scientist or the philosopher may 'attach a definite and limiting force to a term for its use in the given field. But both this simple kind of convention-fixing and the achieved linguistic originalities entailed in the thinking of profound philosophers depend on the central core – without it they couldn't be achieved.'

'Thought, Logic and Objectivity' clinches the argument that Leavis began in his attack on Lord Snow's Rede lecture. Lord

Robbins, unfortunately, shares Snow's belief that there are two cultures: 'To me his diagnosis seems obvious, though it is my experience that the antagonisms he deplores arise chiefly on one side.' 'Obvious' is not what Lord Robbins means, but the clichés and the loose use of language are typical of what he represents. Leavis represents a minority, but his outspokenness should have the effect of encouraging it not to feel impotent.

13 A Visiting Professor

In 1962, when Leavis's three years as University Reader ended, he accepted an Honorary Fellowship at Downing, only to resign it two years later, after the college authorities had disregarded his advice on who should succeed him as Director of English Studies. When he was offered a Chair at another university, he declined, but in 1965, at the age of seventy, he accepted a Visiting Professorship at York.

That the position was offered to him was due to Philip Brockbank, the Professor of English, who had been an undergraduate at Jesus College from 1946–9, working under A. P. Rossiter and attending Leavis's lectures. But they did not meet until 1955, when they were both examiners. When a second Chair of English was created at York, it was offered to Douglas Brown, who died of cancer shortly after accepting, but not before he had agreed that Leavis was the ideal alternative. Lord James, the Vice-Chancellor, could have vetoed the proposal but he was in favour of it. Sixteen years earlier, outspokenly hostile to the English emulation of American methods in Higher Education, he had published *An Essay on the Content of Education*, which had been favourably reviewed in *Scrutiny* by G. H. Bantock. After writing to offer Leavis the position, Brockbank was invited to call on him at Cambridge. Soon afterwards, he accepted.

As 'Visiting Professor' he taught for two terms out of the three, staying in York from Tuesday till Thursday. Generally he would give one lecture and a couple of seminars each week, choosing his subjects to fit in with the rest of the curriculum. At some of his lectures the audience would be swelled to about 500 by visitors from other universities. When they were open to all departments of York University the average attendance would be about 100; less when they were open only to the English Faculty.

The University of York is a self-contained complex of new buildings outside the old walled city, and at the age of seventy it is not easy to adapt either to new places or new rhythms, especially after anchoring a life on one old university city. Leavis had been given an honour and a jolt. He not only responded extremely well to his new

teaching opportunities, there was also an important new burst of
energy in his writing. In 1967 he published *Anna Karenina and Other
Essays*. That *Lectures in America* came out in 1969 was consequent on
the Leavises' visit to the United States in 1966. That *English Literature
in Our Time and the University* also appeared in 1969 was consequent on
his having been invited to deliver the 1967 Clark lectures in Cambridge. But *Dickens the Novelist* was published in 1970, *Nor Shall My
Sword* in 1972, and *The Living Principle* in 1975. So after twelve years
without bringing out a single book, he produced six within nine years.
Anna Karenina and Other Essays is dedicated 'To the University of
York', *Nor Shall My Sword* 'To the York students who gave me a new
Blake with clean margins to write in', and at the end of the fifth
'discourse' in it he happily pays tribute to his new university:

> Here, bearing the name of the historic city, ancient second capital of
> England, is this convincing evidence of modern skill, modern and
> humane architectural intelligence, and modern resources, seeming, on
> its beautifully landscaped site, to grow in its modernity out of the old
> Hall, the old lakeside lawns and gardens and the old timbered grounds.
> It is easy to see that the architects have been guided by an idea that kept
> them in living touch with true and highly conscious academic foresight,
> and that the idea of the university as I have been insisting on it isn't
> merely mine. Where the external presence is so clear a promise of the
> justifying life and reality it is hardly possible to doubt their being
> generated, and prevailing; that is why I take pride in being allowed to
> feel still associated.

After two years as 'Visiting Professor', he became 'Honorary
Visiting Professor', which reduced his commitment and, of course,
his income, which began to depend almost entirely on royalties. He
could now go to York whenever he liked, with expenses paid, to do
whatever teaching he wanted. He would make his proposals a few
weeks before term began, relating them less now to the rest of the
curriculum than to the work he wanted to do for his own books.
York, had, in that sense, become a substitute for *Scrutiny*. His presence
at the university was attracting undergraduates and post-graduate
students from all over the world, especially – in the last few years –
from Australia and South Africa.

More and more strongly Leavis was tending to prefer seminars to
lectures. The ideal attendance would be between six and twelve.
He would get to know the students individually, though not by
name. 'That dark Australian', he would say afterwards, or 'The tall

South African'. Graduate students on the whole were more responsive to him than the new generation of undergraduates, many of whom wanted to talk more than he was prepared to listen. In lectures and seminars, as at informal meetings over a cup of tea, he would be prone to speak at length about his experiences of being treated as an outsider by the cultural establishment and by the Cambridge English Faculty. Students would find this at worst boring and at best irrelevant to their own problems. For them it was almost impossible to realize that he had been an educational revolutionary: he seemed too much like a representative of the established hierarchy, out of sympathy with the idea of student democracy and apprehensive that the new universities were becoming breeding grounds for the Philistinism they ought to be resisting. When the voice of democracy at York demanded pin-tables, the university provided them. Arriving on the campus one morning in the midst of a sit-in, Leavis pushed his way through the demonstrators to the room that still has his name on it. 'There they were,' he complained, 'drunk with malignant righteousness.'

At the beginning of one academic year, a Leavis seminar was announced, intended for first-year students, but so many others came along that the secretary quickly arranged for him to have a lecture room. About a hundred people sat down to hear him speak. Afterwards she asked him whether she had done the right thing. 'It doesn't matter,' he said. 'I pitched it so that only twelve will come next time.' And he was right.

The essay in the *Anna Karenina* book on Conrad's 'The Secret Sharer' was written as a lecture to be delivered at York in 1966. The essay on *Anna Karenina* had been a lecture to the Slavonic Society at Cambridge. It was printed in the first issue of *The Cambridge Quarterly* (Winter 1965/6) but Leavis's relationship with the editorial board rapidly deteriorated. The second issue included a long article by one of the editors, J. M. Newton, on '*Scrutiny*'s Failure with Shakespeare'. Of the other essays in *Anna Karenina*, the one on *The Pilgrim's Progress* had been written as an 'Afterword' to the New American Library edition of 1964; the one on *Adam Bede* had been a Foreword to the Signet edition of 1961; and the one on Mark Twain's *Pudd'nhead Wilson* had been the Introduction to the Chatto and Windus edition of 1955. Two of the essays had been written for *Commentary*: 'The Americanness of American Literature' in 1952, 'T. S. Eliot as Critic' in 1958. 'The Orthodoxy of Enlightenment' had

been written for *The Spectator* in February 1961 during the controversy that followed the trial which vindicated the Penguin publication of *Lady Chatterley's Lover* in an unexpurgated edition. The
Bishop of Woolwich was enthusing about the novel as a celebration of
'holy communion', but Leavis, who had championed it when everyone else was against it, refused to join in the general rejoicing:

> And I will say now that, even it if could be argued that it is a good thing
> for children and teenagers to be able to buy and read it (as they do,
> figuring largely among the million purchasers), the suggestion that the
> book tends to promote respect for the idea of marriage is fantastically
> and perversely false. Lawrence, when he wrote it, had forgotten what
> marriage (as opposed to a liaison) was.

The essay on Conrad's *The Shadow-Line* had been given as a lecture in
Newcastle (1957) and then published in *The Sewanee Review* (1958).
'The Complex Fate' had been written as an Introduction to Marius
Bewley's book (1952) while 'Towards Standards of Criticism' dates
back to 1933, when Leavis wrote it as the Introduction to his
anthology of criticism from *The Calendar*. The other four essays – two
on Henry James, one on Dr Johnson, one on Ezra Pound – had all
appeared in *Scrutiny* between 1944 and 1951. The editing is much
better than in *The Common Pursuit*: with one exception, all the essays
are dated, with details of their original publication.

Of the four *Lectures in America* three were by Leavis. The first looked
back over the 'Two Cultures' controversy; the second was a consid-
eration of 'Eliot's Classical Standing', praising the rhythmic life of his
verse and describing his creative career as 'a sustained, heroic and
indefatiguably resourceful quest of a profound sincerity of the most
difficult kind', but attacking his essay on 'Tradition and the Individual Talent' and his British Academy Lecture on Milton. Leavis's
third lecture comprises his first detailed critique of Yeats since
New Bearings. The comparison of 'Sailing to Byzantium' (1927) and
'Byzantium' (1930) had been one of his favourite subjects for practical criticism during the early fifties. He had briefly made the point
about the inferiority of the later poem in his 1940 *Scrutiny* review of
Yeats's *Last Poems and Plays*, but the detailed comparison he made so
well in his lectures did not find its way into print until this volume
came out in 1969. 'Yeats: the Problem and the Challenge' succeeds
rather well in dove-tailing specific analysis with general considera-
tions towards an assessment of Yeats's standing as a major poet. The

verdict is that too few of his poems rival the greatness of 'Sailing to Byzantium' and 'Among School Children'. Too many of them are too personal: 'The most resolutely literary-critical study of his poetic career entails biography, personalities, public affairs and history.'

It is useful to read this lecture side by side with the fourth Clark lecture, which describes Eliot's 'power which Arnold would have had no difficulty in recognizing as that of a poet – a great poet: the power of giving concrete definition to (that is, of seizing and evoking in words and rhythms) feelings and apprehension – the focal core with the elusive aura – that have seemed to him peculiarly significant elements in his most private experience.' Yeats was incapable of disciplined thought of the kind that was essential to the construction of *Four Quartets* because he lacked 'capacity for intensely private or non-social (or non-currency) experience – which amounts to saying, for bringing to expression in language what language doesn't readily lend itself to.' There is some excellent criticism of Eliot in these lectures and a good recapitulation of the case against Milton, whose 'genius is to be described not merely as *un-* but as *anti-* Shakespearean'. Unfortunately no one would look for these in a book called *English Literature in Our Time and the University*. On the other hand, Leavis's case against the unregenerate materialism of what he calls the Technologico-Benthamite age and against the Labour Party's disastrous acceptance of the Robbins Report would be less urgent without a demonstration of the teaching and the concern that might be unable to survive in the emergent culture. At the same time he was using T. S. Eliot as a means of commenting on the current situation. We must also concede that the quality of his Eliot criticism could not have been so high if he had had to limit himself to writing a book on him.

14 Dickens

In the third Clark lecture Leavis looks forward to *Dickens the Novelist* with the claim that 'if one man may be said to have created the modern novel, it was Dickens . . . The student should know that the line runs from Dickens to D. H. Lawrence.' In the sixth lecture he executes an oddly embarrassing attack on the unfavourable attitude to Dickens which he describes as 'established', but which is identical with the unorthodox attitude that he and Mrs Leavis were adopting in their early books: 'Dickens is of course a genius, but "as soon as he begins to think he is a child": there you have the attitude.' The lecture then attacks 'the truism that Dickens, though of course (we all know) a genius, is merely an entertainer'. Had the Leavises admitted that they were repudiating their earlier view of Dickens, their new book on him would have been all the more welcome. But the Preface suggests that the 1947 essay on *Hard Times* is being revised only in the same way as the earlier version of the essay on *Dombey and Son*, which had appeared in *The Sewanee Review* during 1962 and was now expanded 'in relation to the stated plan and purpose of our book'. In *Scrutiny* and in *The Great Tradition* the first paragraph of the *Hard Times* essay had claimed that the novel was unique among Dickens's output:

> Yet, if I am right, of all Dickens's works it is the one that has all the strength of his genius, together with a strength no other of them can show – that of a completely serious work of art.

In *Dickens the Novelist* this becomes:

> Yet, if I am right, of all Dickens's works it is the one that, having the distinctive strength that makes him a major artist, has it in so compact a way, and with a concentrated significance so immediately clear and penetrating, as, one would have thought, to preclude the reader's failing to recognize that he had before him a completely serious, and, in its originality, a triumphantly successful, work of art.

The last of the three chapters Leavis contributed to the book was titled 'Dickens and Blake: *Little Dorrit*'. As Chichele Lecturer at Oxford in 1964 he had coupled *Little Dorrit* with *Hard Times* under the title 'Dickens, Art and Social Criticism'. Mrs Leavis had lectured on Dickens and Tolstoy at Bristol and Aberdeen and she incorporated this material into the first chapter she wrote: 'Dickens and Tolstoy: The Case for a Serious View of *David Copperfield*'. But she does not seem to have depended primarily on reworking lecture material for the other three chapters she contributed: '*Bleak House*: A Chancery World', 'How We Must Read *Great Expectations*' and 'The Dickens Illustrations: Their Function'. She also added an appendix to one of Leavis's chapters, three appendices to one of her own, and two to another. Altogether she was responsible for nearly two thirds of the book, which covers only six of Dickens's novels in detail, but they have chosen the right six. Once again, the dedication is revealing:

> We dedicate this book to each other as proof, along with *Scrutiny* (of which for twenty-one years we sustained the main burden and the responsibility), of forty years and more of daily collaboration in living, university teaching, discussion of literature and the social and cultural context from which literature is born, and above all, devotion to the fostering of that true respect for creative writing, creative minds and, English literature being in question, the English tradition, without which literary criticism can have no validity and no life.

Reviewing Dickens's 1864–5 novel *Our Mutual Friend*, Henry James called him

> the greatest of superficial novelists . . . It were, in our opinion, an offence against humanity to place Mr Dickens among the greatest novelists . . . He is master of but two alternatives: he reconciles us to what is commonplace, and he reconciles us to what is odd . . . Mr Dickens is a great observer and a great humorist . . . But when he introduces men and women whose interest is preconceived to lie not in the poverty, the weakness, the drollery of their natures, but in their complete and unconscious subjection to ordinary and healthy human emotions, all his humour, all his fancy, will avail him nothing if, out of the fullness of his sympathy, he is unable to prosecute those generalizations in which alone consists the real greatness of a work of art.

Leavis would never have gone quite as far as this in denigrating Dickens, but his 1937 essay on James maintained that no English novelist had outstripped his achievement, and in 1948 *The Great Tradition* pointedly excluded Dickens from the short-list. Twenty-two years later, Leavis's essay on *Little Dorrit* was nearly twice as long as any he had written about a single novel, and he was now in no doubt that Dickens was 'not only a different kind of genius from James, but a genius of a greater kind. The creative life in him flows more freely and fully from the deep sources – the depth, the freedom and the fullness being the conditions of the Shakespearian suppleness. I refer in this comparative way to James because there is good reason for insisting that Dickens is certainly no less a master than James of the subtleties of the inner life – the inner drama of the individual life in its relations with others.' He castigates James's *The Princess Casamassima* for depending parasitically on unconscious memories of *Little Dorrit*. He also alleges that *What Maisie Knew*, which he still acknowledges as a masterpiece, has roots both in *David Copperfield* and in *Little Dorrit*. 'He translated the Little Dorrit situation, the poignant human truth and the irony of which had clearly made a deep impression on him, into terms of a social world (or, rather, stratum) he had observed closely – and with revulsion. . . . James's assured critical bent is that of the decidedly less great artist.' Leavis's anti-Jamesian *volte-face* would have been more acceptable if he had been more willing to take the reader into his confidence about his reasons for his revaluation of Dickens in relation to his previous genealogy of the Great Tradition.

For the serious critic of Dickens the main problem is one of accountancy: an accurate and intelligible balance-sheet has to be presented, giving credit for the abundant flow of comic creativity against debit entries for lapses into the simplifications of the caricaturist and the sentimentality of the melodramatist. George Orwell[1] made a crucial point when he said 'narrowness of vision is in one way a great advantage to him, because it is fatal for a caricaturist to see too much'. John Holloway has said 'Dickens is not at his best in exploring the most inward and genuine of his characters' feelings', and Christopher Ricks[2] has improved on this by rewording it: 'Dickens is at his best in not exploring the most inward of his characters' feelings.' Ricks also makes good use of a quotation from E. H. Gombrich's *Meditations on a Hobby Horse*: 'the cartoonist can mythologise the world of politics by physiognomizing it.' 'In physiognomizing the world,' adds Ricks, 'Dickens was able to mythologize the world without falsifying it.'

Leavis's 1947 essay on *Hard Times* classed it with James's *The Europeans* as a 'moral fable' – the intention being insistent enough for the representative significance of character and plot to be immediately apparent. 'But then,' Leavis goes on, 'intention is often very

[1] 'Charles Dickens' in *Inside the Whale*. 1940.
[2] Review of Angus Wilson's *The World of Charles Dickens* in the *Sunday Times*.

insistent in Dickens, without its being taken up in any inclusive significance that informs and organizes a coherent whole.' In *Dickens the
Novelist* the words 'often very insistent' are replaced by 'in some well-
known places in Dickens's work – and this has been generally thought
of as a Dickensian characteristic – notably insistent'.

Even in its revised form the reading of *Hard Times* is not hard to
reconcile with the old genealogy of the great tradition. Dickens is
'unmistakably possessed by a comprehensive vision, one in which the
inhumanities of Victorian civilization are seen as fostered and sanc-
tioned by a hard philosophy, the aggressive formulation of an
inhumane spirit'. The philosophy is represented by Mr Gradgrind,
'who has brought up his children on the lines of the experiment
recorded by John Stuart Mill as carried out on himself'. While
'remaining that of the great popular entertainer', Dickens's art has 'a
stamina, a flexibility combined with consistency, and a depth'.
Leavis also praises the suppleness of the narrative and the variety in
the dialogue: 'Some passages might come from an ordinary novel.
Others have the ironic pointedness of the school-room scene in so
insistent a form that we might be reading a work as stylized as Jonsonian comedy . . . Others again are "literary", like the conversation
between Gradgrind and Louisa on her flight home for refuge from
Mr James Harthouse's attentions.' I would have thought that 'melodramatic' was a better word than literary for such dialogue as:

> 'I curse the hour in which I was born to such a destiny.'
> He looked at her in doubt and dread, vacantly repeating: 'Curse the
> hour? Curse the hour?'
> 'How could you give me life, and take from me all the inappreciable
> things that raise it from the state of conscious death? Where are the
> graces of my soul? Where are the sentiments of my heart? What have
> you done, O father, what have you done, with the garden that should
> have bloomed once, in this great wilderness here?'[1]

Unlike Bounderby, who is, as Leavis says, 'consistently a Jonsonian
character in the sense that he is incapable of change', Gradgrind 'has
to experience the confutation of his philosophy, and to be capable of
the change involved in admitting that life has proved him wrong'.
This is why Dickens consigns the Gradgrind children to perdition.
Young Tom, who graduates downwards from debt to bank-robbery,
is recognized by his father while playing a comic negro servant in a

[1] Book the Second, Chapter 12.

travelling circus. Louisa is ill-equipped to resist James Harthouse. Leavis notes these developments but fails to question their plausibility or to analyse the means by which Dickens tries to realize them. But Leavis writes well about Sleary, the circus proprietor, about Sissy Jupe, the clown's daughter, and about the superbly well-written sequence in which Louisa tries to make her father commit himself to advising her whether she ought to marry Mr Bounderby. 'It is a triumph of ironic art. No logical analysis could dispose of the philosophy of fact and calculus with such neat finality. As the issues are reduced to algebraic formulation they are patently emptied of all real meaning.'

In his essay on *Dombey and Son* Leavis is again at his best when dealing with the best sequences of the book, such as the fraught conference about how to keep the baby alive after the death of Mrs Dombey. Mr Chick asks: 'Couldn't something temporary be done with a tea-pot?'

> If a solution of the tea-pot kind could have been found, Mr Dombey would have been spared his painful and characteristic inner conflict. Actually, of course, the cruel irony of the situation for Mr Dombey is that, to save the baby's life, what is needed is a living agent, a woman and a mother, and that, if she can be found, she will inevitably, in the nature of the case, be of the lower orders.

As so often, Dickens's ironic imagination is at its best in a situation where pride or self-righteousness is working as a life-denying or dehumanizing force.

Leavis does not make such high claims for the novel as he does for *Hard Times*. He has to concede that there are 'places where the wonderful vitality clearly ran too much to repetitiveness or to the cheapnesses and banalities of Victorian popular art'. But it was Dickens's 'first essay in the elaborately plotted Victorian novel' dealing with a 'major theme' which 'in actuality serves as licence for endless overworked pathos, for lush unrealities of high moral insistence, for childish elaborations of sensational plot, and for all the disqualifying characteristics (a serious theme being proposed) of melodrama – Victorian melodrama. On the other hand, of course, the genial force of Dickens's inexhaustible creativity is also strongly present, in the vigour of the perception and rendering of life, the varied comedy, the vitality of expression as manifested even in the melodramatic high moments and tours de force and in the flights of rhetorical and sentimental art to which we don't respond, at any rate in the massive way proposed to us.' This summarizes the weaknesses and the strengths which are characteristic of Dickens.

Leavis appears to be coming seriously to grips with the problem of how and why Dickens failed to integrate his material: 'Dickens, it is plain, would have told us that the book had a long-pondered unifying theme and was conceived as a whole.' But we cannot help seeing 'that it is certainly not, in its specious totality, the work of that genius which compels our homage in the strong parts. The creative afflatus goes in other, characteristic and large parts of the book with a moral élan that favours neither moral perception nor a grasp of the real.' Taken together, these formulations add up to a more helpful differentiation of the good Dickens from the bad Dickens than anyone else has provided. John Carey has said[1]: 'We could scrap all the solemn parts of Dickens's novels without impairing his status as a novelist.' His humour is 'so interfused with his creative processes that when it fails his imagination seldom survives it for more than a few seconds.' And John Bayley[2] says that Dickens 'seems to have complete confidence that his day-dream world and its inhabitants are as real – perhaps more real – than the stream of facts, decisions and problems that confronted him in the daily process of living.' But it is only by going beyond generalization to a careful comparison of what works with what doesn't that a critic can help the reader towards a solution of the problem.

Unfortunately Leavis seems to lower his standards when looking at a Dickens text. In the scene at the railway terminus[3] when Mr Toodle declines Mr Dombey's offer of money, Leavis analyses the working of the irony without noticing any sentimentality in Dickens's treatment of Toodle. Discussing 'the pages dealing with Paul's education', Leavis says we are given 'childhood with the unique Dickensian vividness, delicacy and truth . . . The genius is an intense concern for the real, and Dickens, when under its command, isn't tempted to sentimentalize.' It seems to me that there is a great deal of falsification in the adult knowingness Dickens imputes to Paul.

> 'Berry's very fond of you, ain't she?' Paul once asked Mrs Pipchin when they were sitting by the fire with the cat.
> 'Yes,' said Mrs Pipchin.

[1] *The Violent Effigy: a Study of Dickens's Imagination.* Faber 1973.
[2] *The Romantic Survival.* Constable 1957.
[3] Chapter XX.

'Why?' asked Paul.

'Why!' returned the disconcerted old lady. 'How can you ask such things, Sir! why are you fond of your sister Florence?'

'Because she's very good,' said Paul. 'There's nobody like Florence.'

'Well!' retorted Mrs Pipchin, shortly, 'and there's nobody like me, I suppose.'

'Ain't there really though?' asked Paul, leaning forward in his chair, and looking at her very hard.

'No,' said the old lady.

'I'm glad of that,' observed Paul, rubbing his hands thoughtfully. 'That's a very good thing.'

Writing of Jenny Wren in *Our Mutual Friend*, Henry James was right to complain: 'Like all Mr Dickens's pathetic characters, she is a little monster . . . she belongs to the troop of hunchbacks, imbeciles, and precocious children who have carried on the sentimental business in all Mr Dickens's novels; the little Nells, the Smikes, the Paul Dombeys.' As children, Pip in *Great Expectations* and David Copperfield are incomparably more lifelike. Leavis is here prone to underline the obvious and too tolerant of the simplifications.

He admits to finding Captain Cuttle boring, but he adds: 'There is an immense deal of Dickens's comic creation that, in its genial and self-justifying liveliness and force, gives us what we acclaim as the expression of his genius, and yet, in the respect referred to, belongs with Captain Cuttle.' He concedes the disparity between 'the real world of Dombey and Son's counting-house' and the make-believe of the happy ending and of Carker's villainy. This 'ethos of unreality' is announced by such sentences as 'A wandering princess and a good monster in a story-book might have sat by the fireside, and talked as Captain Cuttle and poor Florence talked – and not have looked very much unlike them'. Leavis is right to stress Dickens's intelligence, but if he often lapsed below the level it ought to have set for him, the problem is not resolved by asserting 'His distinctive genius was the ability to respond freely and expansively to the inspirations of popular taste, popular tradition and the market, and, in doing so, to evolve for himself (and for the world) a high intellectual art'.

The best of Leavis's three Dickens essays is the one on *Little Dorrit*, and it has come in for some extremely high praise. 'There is no doubt that Leavis has seen more in Dickens that anyone else,' wrote Barbara Hardy.[1] 'His essay on *Little Dorrit* stands with Coleridge on

---

[1] Review of *Dickens the Novelist* in *The New Statesman*, 9 October 1970.

Shakespeare or Eliot on Donne as a profound testimony to imagination . . . To read the analysis of Amy Dorrit's "withdrawingness", Doyce's disinterested scientific energy and its affinity to art or Flora Finching's exuberant sense of reality is to enlarge one's sense of both the novelist's and the critic's range.' Angus Wilson's review of the book praised Leavis's power 'to read more carefully and with fewer preconceptions than any other critic I know (except his wife) . . .[1] I don't think his powers have been seen to better advantage than in his chapter on *Little Dorrit.*'

Of all Dickens's novels it is the least open to Orwell's complaint that 'He is all fragments, all details – rotten architecture, but wonderful gargoyles'. The image of the prison is developed into an architectural principle. The Marshalsea, Venice and Marseilles are the three naves of this prison-cathedral, the attitudes of Calvinist commercialism are the walls, while the motif of the caged bird is strikingly recurrent among the gargoyles. Leavis's main argument is irrefutable. 'What Dickens hated in the Calvinistic commercialism of the early and middle Victorian age – the repressiveness towards children, the hard righteousness, the fear of love, the armed rigour in the face of life – he sums up now in its hatred of art. . . . . The inquest into contemporary civilization that he undertook in *Little Dorrit* might equally be called a study of the criteria implicit in an evaluative study of life.' Leavis insists – as he did when discussing Lawrence – 'that life, for a mind truly intent on the real, is life in the concrete; that life is concretely "there" only in individual lives; and that individual lives can't be aggregated, generalized or averaged'. On the other hand, the great novelist cannot help taking account of 'social conditions, conventions, pressures' – the civilization in which he finds himself. *Little Dorrit*, which was published in monthly instalments between December 1855 and June 1857, starts with the words 'Thirty years ago' because the action has to be set when debt was still punishable by imprisonment, but Dickens was actually writing about the fifties.

[1] That the tribute to Mrs Leavis should be in a parenthesis is characteristic of the treatment she has received. She has written some very fine criticism, which I have not discussed in this book, and it seems outrageous that the university which had her in its midst should not have employed her. Not that the problem she posed was simple. Her life has been complicated by illness, by domestic responsibilities, by having three children and by understandable rancour against the Faculty that disregarded her very considerable achievements. With more income and more encouragement, her critical output could have been much greater.

I think Lionel Trilling was wrong[1] to argue that 'The imagination of *Little Dorrit* is marked not so much by its powers of particularization as by its powers of generalization and abstraction. It is an imagination under the dominion of a great articulated idea.' Leavis is right to insist that in this novel 'there is nothing of the rigidly or insistently schematic' to detract from Dickens's power of breathing individual life into his rich variety of figures. They are less cartoonlike than they were in the early novels, and if he still holds back from exploring the most inward of his characters' feelings, he puts us in a much better position to guess at them. Wyndham Lewis once made a rather silly comparison[2] between Mr Jingle's stream of conversation in *Pickwick* and Mr Bloom's stream of consciousness in *Ulysses*. Harry Stone[3] shows that in Flora Finching, Dickens comes much closer to anticipating Joyce. Flora is 'Dickens's ultimate refinement in the scatter-brained character whose disorganized speech is a direct reflection of disorganized thought'.

> 'I declare,' she sobbed, 'I never was so cut up since your mama and my papa not Doyce and Clennam for this once but give the precious little thing a cup of tea and make her put it to her lips at least pray Arthur do, not even Mr F's last illness for that was of another kind and gout is not a child's affection though very painful for all parties and Mr F a martyr with his leg upon a rest and the wine trade in itself inflammatory for they will do it more or less among themselves and who can wonder, it seems like a dream I am sure to think of nothing at all this morning and now Mines of money is it really, but you must you know my darling because you never will be strong enough to tell him all about it upon teaspoons, mightn't it be even best to try the directions of my own medical man. . . .

Again Leavis is at his best in writing about what is best in the novel, but I would have liked a sharper critical focus on the distinction he draws between Arthur Clennam, the 'decently ordinary person' with whom we identify, and the characters 'who invite the description "Dickensian" – the adjective used in this way implying that they so little fall within the expectation suggested by the word

[1] 1953 Introduction to *Little Dorrit* in The New Oxford Illustrated Dickens series.
[2] *The Art of Being Ruled*, 1926.
[3] 'Dickens and Interior Monologue' in *Philological Quarterly*, January 1959. Reprinted in *Charles Dickens*, Ed. Stephen Wall. Penguin Critical Anthologies.

"realism" that they could occur only in a context boldly or licen-
tiously unrealistic'. Little Dorrit herself is not 'a contrived unreality'
like Little Nell. As Leavis says, Little Dorrit 'emerges for us out of the
situation and the routine of daily life that produced her'. But much
depends on Daniel Doyce, the inventor, the representative of human
creativity and the anti-type of Henry Gowan, the gentlemanly pseudo-
artist. Leavis writes very perceptively – though not very lucidly –
about Henry Gowan's destructiveness: 'knowing deep down that he
doesn't know what, if anything, is real in himself, he is determined to
eliminate all possible tests of reality: the reality of the self he prefers
not to recognize for what it is had better, for others (and himself too),
remain a brilliant and disconcerting equivocation.' But it must be
significant that Gowan is characterized, more or less like Flora
Finching, by letting his speech patterns betray the thinking behind
them; Daniel Doyce's dialogue is less revealing. As Orwell says, 'he
has a peculiar way of moving his thumb, a way characteristic of
engineers. After that, Doyce is firmly anchored in one's memory; but,
as usual, Dickens has done it by fastening on something external.'

The most unacceptable of all Leavis's contentions about Dickens is
that he is a great poet. Would a great poet have invited his biographer
to edit his work? Sending *The Battle of Life* to Forster, Dickens wrote:
'If in going over the proofs you find a tendency to blank verse (I
cannot help it when I am very much in earnest) too strong, knock out
a word's brains here and there!' In the 1947 essay on *Hard Times*
Leavis was already lavishing high praise on 'Dickens's command of
word, phrase, rhythm and image: in ease and range there is surely no
greater master of English except Shakespeare.' In *Dickens the Novelist*
he cites a passage from the description of Rome in *Little Dorrit* to
argue that 'neither George Eliot nor James is a great poet in this
sense – the sense in which we find the description felicitous and
potent when we acclaim this kind of effect as intensely characteristic
of the writer's genius'. Like Henry James, George Eliot is accused of
unconscious derivation from Dickens, though the two sentences
Leavis quotes are not especially memorable:

> Through a repetition of the former Italian scenes, growing more
> dirty and more haggard as they went on, and bringing them to where
> the very air was diseased, they passed to their destination. A fine
> residence had been taken for them on the Corso, and there they took up
> their abode, in a city where everything seemed to be trying to stand
> still for ever on the ruins of something else – except the water, which,

following eternal laws, tumbled and rolled from its glorious multitude of fountains.

Nor is the evocation of Venice which Leavis quotes any more Shakespearean:

> In this crowning unreality, where all the streets were paved with water, and where the death-like stillness of the days and nights was broken by no sound but the softened ringing of church-bells, the rippling of the current, and the cry of the gondolier turning the corners of the flowing streets, Little Dorrit, quite lost by her task being done, sat alone to muse.

In both passages the momentum is rhetorical and the images are hollow-centred, as if contrived on the rebound from a discarded cliché. The rhythms are facile and rather slack. George Eliot's description of Rome in Chapter 20 of *Middlemarch* is both more vivid and more valuable as a reflection of the character's mood.

> Ruins and basilicas, palaces and colossi, set in the midst of a sordid present, where all that was living and warm-blooded seemed sunk in the deep degeneracy of a superstition divorced from reverence; the dimmer but yet eager Titanic life gazing and struggling on walls and ceilings; the long vistas of white forms whose marble eyes seemed to hold the monotonous light of an alien world: all this vast wreck of ambitious ideals, sensuous and spiritual, mixed confusedly with the signs of breathing forgetfulness and degradation, at first jarred her as with an electric shock, and then urged themselves on her with that ache belonging to a glut of confused ideas which check the flow of emotion.

The Leavis who wrote *The Great Tradition* may have been more austere than the Leavis who collaborated with his wife on *Dickens the Novelist*, but the younger man was more willing to give reasons for his preferences.

15   T. S. Eliot

Scrutinizing *Four Quartets* in four essays which fill 110 pages of rather small print in *The Living Principle*, Leavis writes at greater length than ever before on a single work of art. He is a better critic of verse than of fiction because his greatest strength lies in his capacity for concentrated attention on representative detail. The more closely he can approximate to the conditions of practical criticism, the better he writes. The accountancy of these four essays is masterly: against a scrupulous recognition of Eliot's greatness is balanced an accurate analysis of his shortcomings. No one has written better than Leavis about Eliot, and, finally liberated from the limitations of length imposed by the lecture and the essay, he draws dividends from his previous methods of working. This critique could have been written only by a man who had not only been pondering deeply for decades about Eliot's verse but also been discussing it in lectures and seminars. Even if the students said little or nothing, Leavis has profited from making the poetry come alive for them, together with his own valuation of it.

Though the critique makes it easier to give the *Four Quartets* the close reading they call for, it is itself difficult, and before embarking on it the prudent reader will turn back to three earlier discussions of Eliot's verse: 'T. S. Eliot's Later Poetry' in *Education and the University*; 'Eliot's Classical Standing' in *Lectures in America*; and 'Why *Four Quartets* matters in a Technologico-Benthamite age' in *English Literature in Our Time*.

It was in the earliest of these essays (written[1] as a review of 'The Dry Salvages' when it appeared in 1942) that Leavis first described the technique of the poetry from *Ash-Wednesday* onwards as 'a technique for sincerity – for giving "sincerity" a meaning. The preoccupation is with establishing from among the illusions, evanescences and unrealities of life in time an apprehension of an assured reality – a reality that, though necessarily apprehended in time, is not of it.' He noticed that in 'Marina', 'The face, "less clear and clearer", doesn't belong to the ordinary experience of life in time.' The effect of

[1] For *Scrutiny* XI 1, Summer 1942.

a higher reality 'depends upon a kind of co-operative co-presence of the different elements of suggestion, the co-operation being, as the spare and non-logical pointing intimates, essentially implicit, and not a matter for explicit development. What in fact we have is nothing of the order of affirmation or statement, but a kind of tentatively defining exploration.' In 'Burnt Norton', which was to become the first of the *Four Quartets*, 'It is as if the poet were conducting a radical inquiry into the nature and methods of his exploration . . . it seems to me to be the equivalent in poetry of a philosophical work – to do by strictly poetical means the business of an epistemological and metaphysical inquiry.' The central preoccupation is 'with re-creating the concept of "eternity"'. In 'The Dry Salvages', the third poem in the sequence, Eliot was concerned mainly 'with dissolving the habit-created "reality" of routine experience and commonsense, with their protective (and constructive) anaesthesias'. Leavis praised the poetry for its 'extraordinary vitality of language', for its 'marvellous mastery of rhythm' and for 'the extraordinary resource, penetration and stamina with which it makes its explorations into the concrete actualities of experience below the conceptual currency'.

The lecture on 'Eliot's Classical Standing' applauds the earlier poetry for its failure to separate 'the man who suffers' from 'the mind which creates'. In 'Portrait of a Lady', 'the rhythmic life is irresistible' and 'the delicate play of shifting tone' would have been possible 'only in a medium that can suggest (as a Miltonic or Tennysonian or Swinburnian medium cannot) the subtleties of living speech . . . You see, the full waking attention is demanded – is compelled – in this use of language and rhythm.'

But Eliot can 'contemplate the relations between men and women only with revulsion or distaste – unless with the aid of Dante'. Leavis suggests that he 'overvalued what Dante had to offer him', taking less than he could have done from Shakespeare. *The Waste Land* 'offers us a comprehensive survey of the well-springs, the sources of life (which have failed), but the only presence of love is . . . where love is romantically-nostalgically evoked' in the quotation from *Tristan und Isolde* and in the brief hyacinth sequence. The poem which preludes *Ash-Wednesday* is *The Hollow Men*, 'a poem in which there is no protest, no irony and no contemptuous revulsion, except from the self to which there is implicitly imputed something like guilt for a failure in itself. The Eliot of "The Hollow Men" had a desperate need to be able to believe in, to be sure of, something real not himself that should claim allegiance and give meaning.' In *Ash-Wednesday* his technique is so rigorously a technique for sincerity that 'what might seem to be his implicit affirmations of belief or acceptance are made by their total context expressions of a spirit, and contributory to an effect, that could hardly exalt or reassure most of the admirers of *The Rock* or *Murder in the Cathedral*. . . . One would hardly think of calling the religious plays insincere; but the difficult and rare kind of sincerity in question is *not* to be attributed to them.' The rhythms of *Ash-Wednesday* are insistently liturgical and the sensibility is undisguisably Christian, but Eliot maintains a precarious heuristic poise. His concern is 'to discover, by a tentative, exploratory, and wholly unwilful kind of creativeness, scrupulously unassertive, what assurance, what reality, what that can be set against the experience of "death's twilight kingdom", he may hope to establish as the significance portended by the hints and gleams and elusive apprehensions'.

Even in 1967, when he used Eliot as the fulcrum for his Clark lectures, Leavis would not have argued that this poise was maintained throughout the *Four Quartets*, but his valuation of them was still very high. He made the point that there is nothing in *Ash-Wednesday* which 'challenges the full attention of the waking mind in the blunt prose-like way of the opening of "Burnt Norton"'. Comparing 'Difficulties of a Statesman' from *Coriolan* with the beginning of the third section in 'East Coker', Leavis comments that the poet's presence in the later verse 'is much completer and that his undertaking is much more comprehensive and pertinacious'. He also defends 'Burnt Norton' against the suggestion D. W. Harding made[1] that it was abstract. 'In taking the "communication" of the "idea" (I use Harding's words) one goes through a different process from the mastering of a logical disquisition; the whole being is involved, and one is compelled, in the taking, to achieve a new realization of the nature of experience.'

Without retracting this point and without wanting to reduce the claim he had made for the importance of *Four Quartets* to our 'Technologico-Benthamite' period, Leavis arrives in *The Living Principle* at a much more careful evaluation based on a much closer study of the words on the page and the emotions, attitudes and ideas that they organize. In 'Burnt Norton' Eliot's art is still 'essentially heuristic', but Harding's review of 'Little Gidding'[2] had commented on the

[1] In his *Scrutiny* review of the *Collected Poems*, V 2, September 1936.
[2] *Scrutiny* XI 3, Spring 1943.

large part played in Eliot's poetry by repulsion as a motive force. He spoke of 'the pressure of urgent misery and self-disgust'. Leavis now analysed its effects on the poem.

What Eliot himself failed to recognize was that the intensity of his need for impersonality was highly personal. In *The Waste Land* he had already equated selfhood with imprisonment, and in 'Tradition and the Individual Talent' he had described the poet's 'continual surrender of himself to something which is more important'. In *Four Quartets* the dismissal of personality is comprehensive. The attempt is to transcend time in an evocation of eternity. Everything but the 'non-temporal now' is rejected as insignificant:

> Ridiculous the waste sad time
> Stretching before and after.

The closing line of 'Burnt Norton' refers back to the line

> Time before and time after

which occurs twice in the third section's description of passengers on the underground with their

> strained time-ridden faces
> Distracted from distraction by distraction
> Filled with fancies and empty of meaning
> Tumid apathy with no concentration

As Leavis says, 'it is made plain that we are to take the evoked Underground as giving us not merely an aspect of life in time, but life as it must essentially be; temporal life as opposed to the postulated state (for is it imagined – or imaginable?) of being "conscious".' For Eliot

> To be conscious is not to be in time.

He also makes 'consciousness' antithetical to 'flesh', and 'spirit' to 'body'. The poem represents a quest for a reality which is spiritual.

As Leavis argues, 'What he *asserts* about his spiritual quest is worth little; the questing that matters is inseparable from the arduous creativity.' His creative mastery is superbly evidenced by 'the vivid completeness of the immediacy' in his description of the open field in the second paragraph of 'East Coker'. Leavis's analysis shows why the third is less satisfactory. The time-shift is delicately contrived, but the country-folk of pre-industrial England are presented condescendingly:

> Rustically solemn or in rustic laughter
> Lifting heavy feet in clumsy shoes,
> Earth feet, loam feet, lifted in country mirth
>
> . . . .
> Keeping the rhythm in their dancing
> As in their living in the living seasons
> The time of the seasons and the constellations
> The time of milking and the time of harvest
> The time of the coupling of man and woman
> And that of beasts. Feet rising and falling.
> Eating and drinking. Dung and death.

This is the Eliot who praised Baudelaire because 'he was at least able to see that to conceive of the sexual act as evil is more dignified, less boring, than to think of it as the natural, "life-giving", cheery automatism of the modern world'.

That 'human kind cannot bear very much reality' is asserted as if it were axiomatic. In Leavis's judgment, this is to be 'essentially nihilistic'. 'For, the reality that Eliot seeks to apprehend being spiritual, he assumes that the spiritual must be thought of as the absolutely "other" – the antithetically and excludingly non-human. He is doomed to frustration by the inability to recognize the nature of the plight (such inability being a mark of it) that makes the effort of escape to which he dedicates himself seem the only kind that offers hope . . . In *Four Quartets*, for all the creative energy devoted to establishing the approach to apprehending, the painfully developed or enforced offer of apprehension is illusory: the real to be apprehended is nothing.'

'East Coker' also has its Underground sequence. 'The "mental emptiness" in those faces is the spiritual philistinism, the vacuity, of the civilization they represent. But "growing terror of nothing to think about" – that, surely is unacceptable; it doesn't belong to their case at all. . . . Curiously enough, as if there were no difference, Eliot slides evenly from *their* "mental emptiness" to that which he is prescribing for himself in a tradition of spiritual discipline:

> Or when, under ether, the mind is conscious but conscious of nothing –
> said to my soul, be still . . .

Not that the mode of the poem is discursive or logical. As Leavis remarked apropos the beginning of 'Burnt Norton', Eliot 'is prepared for frequent abrupt transitions of a kind disconcerting to anyone who feels he has a right to require some familiar form of continuity'. The overall title suggests a musical structure, and '"Music" is the licence Eliot takes to defy the criteria we implicitly expect to be observed in (one can reasonably say) all forms of written English'. The music of the sounds and rhythms is both pleasing and persuasive: often it induces us not to press too hard for answers to questions about relationships. In 'Burnt Norton' there are several statements about 'the pattern', 'the dance' and 'the still point' but, like their relationship, the meaning of each term seems to vary, and Leavis concludes that Eliot himself is not in possession of answers to the questions, though it is not until 'The Dry Salvages' that inconsistency in the use of the word 'pattern' becomes obvious. Not that he is 'deliberately playing false', but unlike Leavis, Eliot, who was at pains to avoid giving offence, cultivated what Leavis calls 'an equivocal subtlety of formulation'. His obituary of Robert Bridges was cleverly worded 'to satisfy the institutionalist *bien-pensants* while making the undisturbed dismissive judgment plain to readers like myself'. As he proceeded with *Four Quartets* his 'technique for sincerity' became less reliable.

The problem of honesty was exacerbated by his disbelief in fact. The second paragraph of 'The Dry Salvages' is aimed at dissolving the familiar divisions between land and sea, present and past, internal and external. Eliot wants to 'generate an acute sense that we are, and can be, at home nowhere'. He 'can't believe in the reality of any humanly created world, or in the human responsibility that maintains one, and the second paragraph continues and sharpens the reminder of what men "choose to forget", which is the unreality of what seems to give significance to the familiar world they live in'. His evocation of time is intended to be 'so disconcerting in its actual experienced diversities and paradoxes that the commonsense assumption of a normal common time, constituent of a real common reality, is badly discredited'. The tenor of 'The Dry Salvages' is to insist that our memories of the past are all deceptive. Only at its point of intersection with timelessness can time yield anything but illusion or the recognition of human nullity. 'The bone's prayer to Death its God' in the second section is reminiscent of the scattered bones in *Ash-Wednesday*, which sang

We are glad to be scattered, we did little good to each other.

But Eliot no longer feels obliged to hold back from making affirmations. In the fourth section of 'East Coker' the references to Original

Sin and Purgatory are unmistakable: Leavis's marginal note was 'Unambiguously committed now – explicitly – to what he was moving towards. But what Christianity is this?' In the second section of 'The Dry Salvages', the

Clamour of the bell of the last annunciation

prefigures

the hardly, barely prayable
Prayer of the one Annunciation.

Even if Eliot now feels he has earned the right to affirm his faith, what can he offer to apprehend when he wishes to reject everything that is contained within time? As Leavis says, 'a conception of pure non-human otherness can hardly be a conception; it can be no more than the ghost of one – a mere postulate. The space cleared for the Other by the elimination of all that "human kind" can recognize as life, value and significance is a vacuum; nothing is left to qualify it. It is not, of course, as vacuous that he offers it. The phrase, "a life-time's death in love", like the equivocal play with the word "action", exemplifies the subtlety with language that enables his need-impelled genius, servant of the dividedness in him as it is, to deceive itself in the essential way, and substitute the illusion of (necessarily) human signi-cance for the vacuum that – if we take the insistent challenge to conclude seriously about the offered thought – he has actually created.'

It is not surprising that the last of the *Four Quartets*, 'Little Gidding' is the weakest, despite the strength of the *terza rima* passage, with its Dantesque evocation of uncanny silence in London during the Blitz. Again Leavis quotes from Harding's favourable reaction to the poem: 'With the sun blazing on the ice, the idea of pentecostal fire, of central importance in the poem, comes in for the first time, an intense, blinding promise of life and (as later passages show) almost unbearable.' As Leavis infers, the word 'poem' here must mean the whole of the *Four Quartets*, and it is odd that Harding does not see it as a sign of weakness that a theme of central importance should be introduced so late. What matters still more is that the three previous quartets have not effectively prepared the ground. There has been no organic growth within the musical structure. The final affirmations do not arise with any conviction of inevitability out of what has pre-ceded them.

Eliot was fifty-four in 1942 when he wrote the section that begins

> Let me disclose the gifts reserved for age
>   To set a crown upon your lifetime's effort.

The three gifts are 'the cold friction of expiring sense without enchantment';

> the conscious impotence of rage
> At human folly, and the laceration
> Of laughter at what ceases to amuse

and

> the rending pain of re-enactment
> Of all that you have done, and been; the shame
> Of motives late revealed, and the awareness
> Of things ill done and done to others' harm
> Which once you took for exercise of virtue.

Leavis was almost eighty when he responded: 'This is the Eliotic fear of life, the recoil from decay and inevitable death.' Even the most masterly achievements of a great critic cannot be compared with a flawed masterpiece by a great poet, but at least a critic can demonstrate why an aged eagle should stretch its wings.

Life and Work – a Table of Dates

Time and the University. Honorary Visiting Professor at York.
Anna Karenina and Other Essays.

1969   Visiting Professor at University of Wales. Published *English
           Literature in Our Time and the University* and *Lectures in America.*
           (With Q. D. Leavis)

1970   Churchill Visiting Professor at Bristol University
           Dickens the Novelist (with Q. D. Leavis)

1971   Began to contribute to *The Human World*

1972   *Nor Shall My Sword*

1974   *Letters in Criticism* (edited by John Tasker)

1975   *The Living Principle*

1976   *Thought, Words and Creativity*

Bibliographies

1. Analytical Bibliography of Leavis's Books

The titles of the books are not always self-explanatory. It is therefore necessary to tell the reader where to look for what. The books are published by Chatto and Windus.

The numbers following the titles refer to the relevant pages of this book which discuss the work in question.

1930 *Mass Civilization and Minority Culture*, 5, 11, 13, 15, 64
 D. H. Lawrence, 11, 84
1932 *New Bearings in English Poetry*, 9, 19, 20, 24, 31, 49, 65, 111
 Poetry and the Modern World, 24
 The Situation at the End of the War, 25-6
 T. S. Eliot, 26-8
 Ezra Pound, 27-30, 39
 Gerard Manley Hopkins, 30
 How to Teach Reading: a Primer for Ezra Pound, 21, 31-3, 64, 67
1933 *For Continuity*, 21
 Marxism and Cultural Continuity
 Mass Civilization and Minority Culture
 The Literary Mind
 What's Wrong with Criticism?
 Babbitt Buys the World
 Arnold Bennett: American Version
 John Dos Passos
 D. H. Lawrence
 D. H. Lawrence and Professor Irving Babbitt
 'Under which King, Bezonian?'
 Restatements for Critics
 'This Poetical Renascence'
 Joyce and 'The Revolution of the Word'
 Culture and Environment (with Denys Thompson), 21, 22, 65, 111
 Towards Standards of Criticism. Selections from *The Calendar of Modern Letters*, 1925-27. Edited with an Introduction, 21, 122
1934 *Determinations*: Critical Essays. Edited with an Introduction. Selected from the first 6 issues of *Scrutiny*, 21, 22, 50

Antony and Cleopatra and *All for Love*, 80, 90–1
Four Quartets, 139–44
1976 *Thought, Words and Creativity*
contains analyses of D. H. Lawrence's *The Plumed Serpent,
Women in Love, The Captain's Doll* and *The Rainbow*.

2. Select Bibliography of Uncollected Essays and Reviews

1929 'T. S. Eliot – A Reply to the Condescending' in *The Cambridge Review*, February. Reprinted in *The Cambridge Mind*, Eds. Eric Homberger, William Janeway and Simon Schama, Cape.

1935 'Dr Richards, Bentham and Coleridge', review of *Coleridge on Imagination* by I. A. Richards in *Scrutiny* III, March 1935.
'Marianne Moore', review of *Selected Poems* by Marianne Moore in *Scrutiny* IV, June 1935.

1936 'Mr Auden's Talent', review of *Look Stranger* by W. H. Auden, *The Ascent of F.6* by W. H. Auden and Christopher Isherwood in *Scrutiny* V, December 1936.

1937 'The Recognition of Isaac Rosenberg', review of *The Complete Works of Isaac Rosenberg*, ed. D. W. Harding and Gordon Bottomley in *Scrutiny* VI, September 1937.

1938 'Revaluations (XI): Arnold as Critic' in *Scrutiny* VII, December 1938.

1939 'Hart Crane from this Side', review of *The Collected Poems of Hart Crane* in *Scrutiny* VII, March 1939.

1940 'Revaluations (XIII): Coleridge in Criticism' in *Scrutiny* IX, June 1940;
'Hardy the Poet' in *Southern Review* vi, 1940–41.

1942 'After *To The Lighthouse*', review of *Between the Acts* by Virginia Woolf in *Scrutiny* X, January 1942.

1945 'Metaphysical Isolation' in *Gerard Manley Hopkins* by the Kenyon Critics. New Directions, Norfolk 1945.

1957 'The Critic's Task, review of *The Energies of Art* by Jacques Barzun in *Commentary*, July 1957.

1959 'Romantic and Heretic', review of *D. H. Lawrence: a Composite Biography* Volume III in *The Spectator*, 6 February.

1960 'Lawrence After Thirty Years', Address at the University of Nottingham. Printed in *D. H. Lawrence*, ed. H. Coombes. Penguin Critical Anthologies 1973.

1961 'Genius as Critic', review of *Phoenix: The Posthumous Papers of D. H. Lawrence* in *The Spectator*, 24 March 1961.

1963 'James as Critic', Introduction to *Henry James: Selected Literary Criticism* ed. Morris Shapira. Heinemann, London.

1972 'Justifying One's Valuation of Blake', Lecture at Bristol University. Printed in *The Human World*, No. 7, May.

1973 'Memories of Wittgenstein' in *The Human World*, No. 10, February.

1974 '"Believing in" the University' in *The Human World*, Nos. 15–16, May – August.

1976 'Mutually Necessary' in *New Universities Quarterly*, March.

3. Select Bibliography of Critical Writing on Leavis

1933 Marshall McLuhan, 'Poetic v. Rhetorical Exegesis: the Case for Leavis against Richards and Empson' in *Sewanee Review*, April.

1949 Martin Greenberg, 'The Influence of Mr Leavis' in *Partisan Review*, XVI, 8 August.

1952 I. Gregor, 'The Criticism of F. R. Leavis' in *Dublin Review*, No. 457.
M. Jarrett-Kerr, 'The Literary Criticism of F. R. Leavis' in *Essays in Criticism*, II, 4.

1957 Lionel Trilling, 'Dr Leavis and the Moral Tradition' in *A Gathering of Fugitives*. Secker.
W. W. Robson, 'Mr Leavis on Literary Studies' in *Universities Quarterly*, XI, February.
Donald Davie, 'F. R. Leavis's *How to Teach Reading*', *Essays in Criticism*, July.

1959 Vincent Buckley, *Poetry and Morality: Studies on the Criticism of Matthew Arnold, T. S. Eliot and F. R. Leavis*. Chatto.
Raymond Williams, *Culture and Society. 1780–1950*. Chatto.
R. Williams, R. J. Kaufmann, A. Jones, 'Our Debt to Dr Leavis – A Symposium' in *Critical Quarterly*, Autumn.

1960 J. Bourne, 'The Loneliness of the Long Distance Runner' in *The Guardian*, 8 April.

1962 George Steiner, 'Men and Ideas: F. R. Leavis' in *Encounter*, May. (Essay reprinted in *Language and Silence*. Faber 1967.)

1963 C. D. Narasimhaiah (ed.), *F. R. Leavis: Some Aspects of his Work*. Rao and Raghavan, Mysore.

1964 René Wellek, 'The Literary Criticism of Frank Raymond Leavis' in *Literary Views: Critical and Historical*, ed. Carroll Camden. Chicago University Press.
George Watson, *The Literary Critics: A Study of English Descriptive Criticism*. Chatto.
William Walsh, *A Human Idiom: Literature and Humanity*.

1966 Andor Gomme, *Attitudes to Criticism*. Southern Illinois University Press.
John Casey, *The Language of Criticism*. Methuen.
David Lodge, *Language of Fiction: Essays in Criticism and Verbal Analysis of the English Novel*. Routledge.
1969 John Gross, *The Rise and Fall of the Man of Letters*. Weidenfeld.
1973 Ian Robinson, *The Survival of English: Essays in criticism of language*. Cambridge University Press.
1974 Clive James, *The Metropolitan Critic*. Faber.
1975 'Leavis at 80 – what has his influence been?' in *The Listener*, 24 July. A Symposium edited by Philip French with contributions from D. W. Harding, L. C. Knights, M. C. Bradbrook and others.
'F. R. Leavis; b. 1895: "Stability and Growth"' in *The New Universities Quarterly* XXX 1. Winter. Contributions by Michael Tanner, Andor Gomme, Michael Black, Fred Inglis, David Holbrook and others.

For a complete bibliography of writings by and about Leavis up to 1964 see D. F. McKenzie and M-P. Allum. *F. R. Leavis. A Check-List 1924–1964*. Chatto 1966.

Index